TEXAS IN 1776

WEST TEXAS LIBRARY SYSTEM
1306 9th St./Lubbock, Texas 79401

This material provided by the West Texas
Library System with a grant from the
Texas State Library through the Texas
Library Systems Act (H.B. 260) and the
Library Services and Construction Act
(P.L. 91-600).

TEXAS IN 1776

A HISTORICAL DESCRIPTION

SEYMOUR V. CONNOR

JENKINS PUBLISHING CO.
AUSTIN/1975

CONTENTS

PROLOGUE

1

The Independence of the British colonies was declared in 1776; the fighting that brought on that declaration began in 1775; the Anglophobia that led to the fighting developed after the Seven Years' War. With the beautiful clarity provided by the selective lenses in the long telescope of time, historians see a train of events following that war which seems almost inevitably to have led to the American Revolution. A concurrent series seems, not as obviously, to have led to a consolidation and strengthening of the Spanish colonies in North America. By the end of the American Revolution, Spain appeared to be in a position to dominate, if not ultimately to control, the entire continent. Such was not to be its destiny, but in the two decades of the development and culmination of the American Revolution, Spain colonized California, expanded in Arizona and New Mexico, extended her frontiers along the Mississippi, and consolidated her posts in Texas. Although Texas lost its basic importance to Spanish officials as a buffer against France, the settlements there were to grow stronger and even somewhat prosperous. Indeed, on the eve of the American Revolution, Texas was on the brink of becoming a vital, if not a thriving, colonial entity.

The Seven Years' War, which seems to have sparked these colonial changes, started as the French and Indian War in 1754 when George Washington unsuccessfully attempted to dislodge some French traders from the head of the Ohio River in western Pennsylvania. The fighting spread between British and French colonists and grew into a general European conflict in 1756 following the crystallization of alliances between Britain and Prussia, and France and Austria. The war went badly for Britain at first, but from 1757 to 1761 William Pitt directed a war effort that brought defeat to France, with stirring victories by James Wolfe in Canada and Robert Clive in India. On the verge of capitulation, France formed the "Family Compact" and dragged a reluctant Spain into the war. There were Bourbons then on the thrones of both nations. Although Pitt was fired by George III, his war machine quickly seized vital Spanish colonial bases in Florida, Cuba, and the Philippines, and even threatened French power on the European continent. To avoid destruction, France and her allies sued for peace. The Treaty of Paris of 1763 formalized the British victory.

It was this treaty that reshaped the map of North America and thus changed the course of history. Spain had to give Florida to England in order to get back her colonial posts. France lost almost her entire colonial empire in India and Africa, as well as in North America. Before the war, France had claimed the whole Mississippi drainage area—the heart of North America—plus all of present Canada save for a small region around Hudson Bay surrendered to England in a previous war. To prevent her centuries-long enemy from controlling all of her lost empire, and partly to compensate her Catholic cousins for their anticipated loss of Florida, France ceded that part of Louisiana west of the Mississippi to Spain in a secret concord a few months prior to the treaty. Britain ratified the transfer at the time of the treaty to avoid further conflict.

Thus was over a hundred years of colonial imperialism by England, Spain, France, Holland, and Sweden narrowed down in North America to England and Spain. England "owned" all of the continent east of the Mississippi plus modern Canada. Spain "owned" everything west of the river. Neither power actually occupied much of its territory. Both had to deal with erstwhile Frenchmen within their new colonial boundaries, with restless Indian tribes, and with the financial burdens of the war and their expanded frontiers. Consequently both England and Spain revised their colonial policies.

In a now-familiar cascade of parliamentary bungling (from the American view) Britain issued the Proclamation of 1763, followed by the Sugar Act, the Stamp Act, the Quebec Act, the Townshend Duty Acts, the Tea Act, and the Intolerable Acts, each of which stiffened further the resistance of the colonists. The First Continental Congress met in 1774, the very fact of its assembling almost an unwritten statement of independence. So challenged, Britain closed colonial ports and postured military control. It took but a small spark in the gathering tension to ignite powder and shot at Lexington in April 1775.

In the readjustment after the Treaty of Paris of 1763, Spain's problems were rather similar to Britain's, but her solutions had entirely different results. Of course, the troublesome Plains Indians did not have a leader of the magnitude of Pontiac; there was no religious conflict with the Frenchmen now within her empire; like Spain, France's judicial institutions had been based on the magisterial Roman Law, so this caused no need for a Spanish Quebec Act; Spanish colonists were accustomed to heavy taxation and autocratic government, so new regulations brought no resentment; and Spain's monarch, although of alien family like the Hanovarian George III of England, was no bumbler. Charles III of Spain (a Bourbon prince) was energetic and brought new leadership to the Spanish empire. Reforms were effected in Spain itself and throughout her dominions. That Charles III's reforms grew out of personal inspections and recommendations by competent men is one of the major differences between Britain's post-war policies and Spain's. On the northern frontier these reforms were the result of two quite thorough inspections made by José de Gálvez with an emphasis on financial aspects of the empire and by the Marqués de Rubí primarily for military purposes.

Gálvez was the second son of an impoverished branch of a distinguished family. Fluent in French (and married to a Frenchwoman), Gálvez won favor at the Bourbon court in Madrid after Charles III's ascension. He was appointed *visitador-general* of New Spain in 1765 and toured the vice-royalty from 1765 to 1772 when he returned to Spain. His rewards for meritorious service were further honors and posts under Charles III, most connected with colonial administration. Although he never visited Texas, and Sonora was as close as he came to the American Southwest, his visitation and recommendations contributed heavily to frontier changes.

Rubí was the son of Francisco Pignatelli, one-time Spanish ambassador to France, and María Francisca Rubí Corbera y San Climent, a Spanish noblewoman from whom he inherited his titles, Baron of Llinas and Marqués de Rubí. Rubí was already a prominent figure in Spanish politics when Charles III came to Spain in 1759; after his service on the northern frontier, 1767-1769, he returned to Madrid. Although he was a distinguished and important man in his own time, he entered the pages of history only because of his military inspection of the northern frontier.

The results of these two inspections and the recommendations of Gálvez and Rubí, together with other recommendations via the Council of the Indies, were broad-based and sweeping reforms. Those directly affecting Texas during the period of the American Revolution were the abandonment of East Texas; the closing of the western missions and the San Sabá presidio; the reform in the administration of the presidios; a new Indian policy based on alliances with the Comanches; the transfer of the Queréteran missions to the supervision of the *colegio* at Zacatecas as a result of the expulsion of the Jesuits; the creation of the *Provincias Internas;* and, most significant of all, the opening of legal commerce (especially in cattle) with Louisiana.

Thus, Texas in 1776 was totally unlike the missionary outpost it had been a short decade earlier. The changes that occurred during the 1770's were among the most radical that have ever taken place in Texas in so brief a period of time.

MAP 1

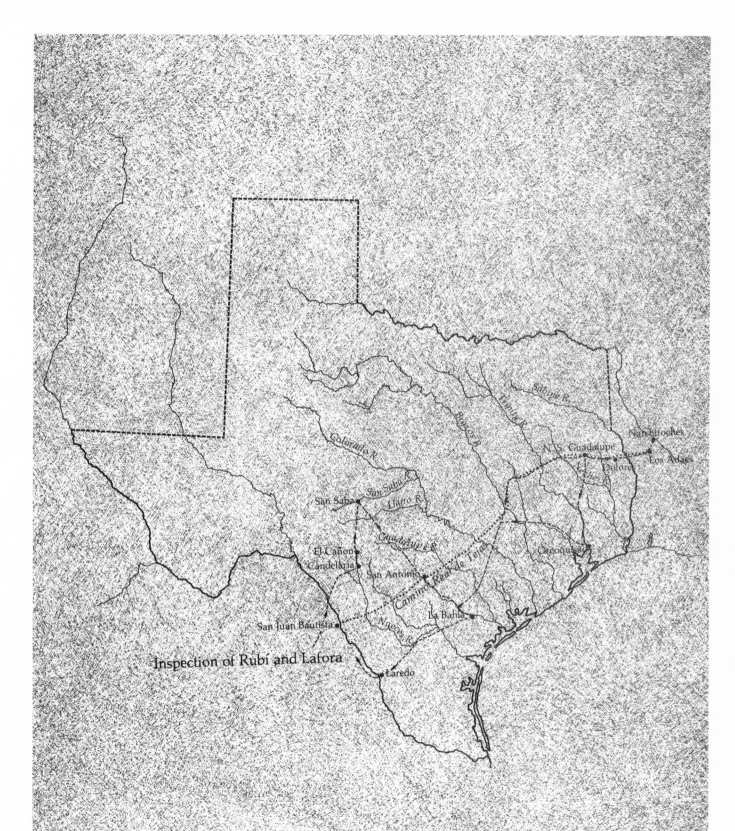

Inspection of Rubí and Lafora

THE PRESIDIOS

2

Cayetano María Pignatelli Rubí Corbera y San Climent, Marqués de Rubí and Baron de Llinas, arrived in Mexico City in December 1765. He could have described the capital of the viceroyalty as the most cosmopolitan and civilized metropolis in the New World, for such it was, as well as the richest, largest, and most urbane. It would be at least a century before any city in the British colonies could rival the splendor of its many churches (the great cathedral was then nearing completion), its library, university, theater, and other magnificent buildings, not the least of which was the viceregal palace and government offices, occupied at that time by the Marqués de Cruillas. Rubí, who spent three months in Mexico City waiting for additional instructions from Cruillas, chafed at the delay.

He left, finally, in mid-March 1766 and proceeded with the major portion of his entourage to Durango where he arrived on April 11. A few days later he was joined by the remainder of his party, which included the man who was to be the most important of the entire group, Don Nicolás de la Fora (or Lafora, as the name is usually rendered). Lafora, who was a captain of engineers, kept a meticulous daily journal of the expedition, drew sketches of the presidios that Rubí inspected, and compiled a map of the entire northern frontier.

Rubí's inspection tour was made in three loops: north from Durango via Chihuahua City to El Paso and into New Mexico; west from the Chihuahua-El Paso road into Sonora and present Arizona, returning south through the Yaqui country to cross the road he had traveled from Durango to Chihuahua City; finally, northwest by way of Saltillo to cross the Rio Grande above present Eagle Pass and thence across Texas to Los Adaes in present Louisiana. It was an incredible journey, covering nearly 8,000 miles in 20 months. At each presidio he visited, he followed generally the same inspection routine. He held a formal or semiformal inspection of troops and horses, and checked the physical condition of the buildings, while Lafora and his assistant, José de Urrutia, made a ground plan. He then interviewed various individual soldiers about their duties, their provisions, and their pay. He was to find soldier morale uniformly low, with the troops usually being charged exorbitant prices for the supplies sold to them by the presidio commanders. Since the accounts for these charges were usually greater than their salaries, little or no pay ever reached the individual soldiers. Rubí also audited the books of the presidio commanders and found the soldiers' plight readily verifiable on the ledgers. In many cases he found that the officers cheated on the amounts charged the men. Conditions in Texas were among the worst encountered on the entire tour.

Rubí and Lafora crossed the Rio Grande into Texas on July 16, 1767, a few miles above San Juan Bautista (across and up river from present Eagle Pass), which he visited on his return to Mexico on November 22. To get across the river they borrowed a crudely made canoe from a ranchería of Lipan Apache Indians nearby. The crossing was difficult because of the swiftness of the flow at that point. One man, a Pausan Indian, was drowned, and two horses were lost. They did not get their baggage across the river until the following morning, July 17. These problems were but precursors of what was to be the most arduous part of their twenty-month journey.

But the first week was spent traveling at a leisurely pace almost due north through the loveliest scenery Texas has to offer—the hills of the eastern edge of the Edwards Plateau. Passing near present Brackettville, they reached the little Candelaria Mission on the upper Nueces near present Montell on the night of July 18. There they found only a house for the Franciscan padres, a tiny chapel, and a large hut for Lipan Indians who came and went, but never remained for long. The Lipans only laughed at the fathers, said Lafora, for their fruitless zeal. A modern Texan cannot help but wonder whether indeed it was religious evangelism that brought the brown-robed friars to one of the most beautiful natural vacationlands in the entire Southwest, where the sparkling clear waters of the spring-fed upper Nueces and its tributaries abounded in fish. There is no particular record of the padres' zeal at angling.

The next day the expedition shifted about 10 miles to the settlement known as El Cañon. There they found an officer with a detachment of thirty troops from the presidio on the San Sabá, another small chapel, and two "useless" missionaries. Lafora, the engineer, was disgusted. There were two, three-pound cannons not only mounted on carriages that would not function, but also without anything to fire them with. The priests called the mission San Lorenzo de la Santa Cruz. Located at present Camp Wood, the mission site was excavated by the state archeologist a few years ago. Both Candelaría and El Cañon were apparently made of logs and the ancillary buildings of stick and mud wattle called *jacal*.

The visitors spent an extra day at this delightful place and then proceeded to the presidio on the San Saba River which was almost due north about 100 miles overland and three and a half days' travel. The whole route was vulnerable to Comanche attack, and Lafora felt that the hostiles were constantly watching them for stragglers. Comanches were indeed in the vicinity, for the next day the Spaniards saw the smoke of signal fires and found tracks. They remained in the safety of the presidio from July 25 to August 4 when Rubí determined to continue. During this time there were several Indian alarms, but no hostile Indian was actually seen. Lafora reported a complement of 100 mounted men. Seven cannons adorned the walls, none of which was serviceable. Neither Lafora nor Rubí thought the place was worth what it cost to maintain.

This presidio had been sturdily built of stone ten years earlier to protect the San Sabá de la Santa Cruz Mission, also built in 1757,

but it was about a mile from the mission and on the opposite side of
the river. When the Comanches brutally attacked in 1758, the troops
at the presidio were helpless to prevent the massacre. The mission,
built of wood, was burned, and today there are no visible remains.
The site is marked in downtown Menard by a Texas Centennial Commission marker. The presidio, which fell into ruins, was reconstructed
in 1936 without benefit of archeological research or reference to the
sketches made by Lafora. This sad restoration is now itself a ruin,
located at the edge of the golf course west of Menard.

It took the expedition five days to travel from the presidio at
present Menard to San Antonio. Many a modern Texan would love to
have accompanied these Spaniards on this trip through the then un-
spoiled Texas hill country. It is a delight even to imagine it: they
camped at the junction of the Llano and the San Saba; at the head of
the Pedernales; on the upper Guadalupe; and on Balcones Creek!

San Antonio, founded in 1718 by Martín de Alarcón and
Father Antonio de San Buenaventura Olivares, was the most important Spanish settlement in Texas. But Lafora wrote disparagingly of it.
There were only 16 families of Canary Islanders (imported in 1731) at
the town and 22 soldiers. The soldiers spent most of their time on
guard duty at the nearby missions, of which there were five. The presidio, built by Alarcón and rebuilt by Aguayo in 1722, was worthless.
The inspectors found over eight hundred Indians and ten missionaries
at the missions. Lafora thought that the missions, which he said were
rich, could be self-supporting instead of a drain on the royal treasury
and that there was no need for the Crown to support troops at San.
Antonio since there were enough mission Indians for defense.

The expedition moved on to Los Adaes on August 25, which
was then the capital of Texas. Curiously, these travelers did not
follow the Camino Real de Texas, the established road from San Antonio to Nacogdoches. It may be inferred that Comanche marauders
may have made that route too dangerous. Whatever the reason, they
left San Antonio by the road to La Bahía, then cut eastward to inter-
sect the road connecting La Bahía to East Texas and followed it. That
road, apparently infrequently used, was overgrown with brush, reduced to a bad, narrow path that often was blocked by fallen trees.
The stream crossings were difficult. At length, after twelve days of
arduous travel, they reached the Guadalupe Mission at what had once
been the Caddoan village of Nacogdoche. They found only one padre

at the mission and not a single Indian. Nor had there ever been an Indian at the mission, the friar told them, in the forty years of its existence. Living nearby were two soldiers on the royal payroll and their families. Several young men appeared to be farming in the immediate area. It was to this unencouraging place a dozen years later that Gil Ybarbo led several hundred people to establish the third enduring Spanish settlement in Texas. The Rubí entourage rested there one day before moving on toward Los Adaes.

On the way they passed the Dolores mission south of present San Augustine. It was of as little worth, said Lafora, as the Guadalupe mission, but more costly, since the crown bore the costs of two padres and a lay brother, as well as two soldiers and their families. The Ais Indians of the vicinity never came into the mission. Two days later, on September 10, Rubí and Lafora reached Los Adaes.

The capital of Texas (in present eastern Louisiana about 15 miles southwest of Natchitoches) was at that time more impressive a settlement than San Antonio. There were sixty soldiers at the presidio (Pilar), commanded by the governor of Texas who resided there. The adjacent mission (San Miguel) had two priests whose only job was to minister to the soldiers, since the Adaes Indians also shunned mission life. Both the presidio and the mission, like the others in East Texas, were built of logs. The presidio was a stockade in the shape of a hexagon, the walls surmounted by six brass cannons. Lafora found the logs rotten and in many places the wall in ruins. Although he did not mention them, there were several hundred families living in and around Los Adaes. Rubí's own report estimated thirty families, but an account a few years later put the population at over five hundred. Some were in their second generation in Texas. It was a farming community, with chickens, pigs, cows, sheep, cultivated fields, and orchards. For years before the transfer of Louisiana in 1763, these settlers had carried on an illegal trade with both the Indians of East Texas and the French at nearby Natchitoches. Although it served as the capital of Texas for a half-century, there exists not even an inadequate description of the settlement of Los Adaes, and nothing remains of it today save for a few lines in the history books.

The inspection party tarried there for two weeks and then struck out for the settlement of Orcoquisac. Retracing their steps to Nacogdoches, they turned south through almost impassable thicket and swamp, being rained on every day of the eight-day trip, probably the worst traveling of the entire 8,000-mile tour of the frontier. The settlement at Orcoquisac had been founded in 1757 because of a report that there were French traders operating in the area. The report was never verified, and the settlement plans never came to full fruition. It was planned to be a mission for the Orcoquisa Indians, a presidio of a hundred troops, and a civil settlement of an equal number of families. Floods in the area caused a relocation of the mission. The presidial stockade may never have been completed, and few civilians ever moved to the area. Rubí and Lafora found two priests at the mission and thirty-one soldiers at the presidio. The exact location of the settlement was not known until about ten years ago when a copy of the Lafora sketch turned up at the British Museum. Interstate Highway 10 cuts right through one edge of the site, just east of the Trinity River in present Chambers County. An archeological excavation was made of what remained.

Orcoquisac had had a stormy and unhappy existence. Because of the difficult access to it, it was almost impossible to supply. Frequently the priests and soldiers were reduced to eating roots and wild fruit. In 1764 after the arrival of a new commander named Rafael Martínez Pacheco whom the troops considered arrogant and ill-tempered, there was a mutinous uprising, and all but four or five soldiers deserted. The governor, who resented the fact that Pacheco was independent of his authority, came down from Los Adaes to investigate the charges. Pacheco barricaded himself in the fort, and after brief fighting, it was put to the torch and at least partially destroyed. Pacheco fled in the excitement. It was an ignominious episode in Texas frontier history.

After Orcoquisac, there remained only one further post in Texas to inspect. The party moved out for La Bahía without much hope of finding a good road. First they had to cross the Trinity, then swollen by the recent rains, and traverse the swampy marshlands north of Galveston Bay. Finally they reached the road between La Bahía and Nacogdoches—the one Lafora had thought so bad when they went out on it. It had not improved any, but Lafora's perspective had changed. In all it took sixteen days to reach La Bahía. They remained there from November 1 to November 11.

At La Bahía they found two missions, operated by three Franciscans; a presidio garrisoning fifty soldiers, including officers; and forty-six civil settlers. The first of the two missions was Espíritu

Santo, which had been founded by Aguayo and Ramón in 1722 on the site of La Salle's Fort St. Louis and moved in 1727 to the Guadalupe River and again in 1749 to its location at present Goliad. The other was Rosario, established in 1754 about five miles upstream. Espíritu Santo has been restored as a state park; only a few ruins remain of Rosario. The presidio, called Loreto, has also been restored and is the property of the Catholic Church. Loreto has had one of the longest and most exciting histories of any place in Texas, second only to the Alamo. Its major purpose during the Spanish era was not only to give protection to the padres, but also to stand as a bastion guarding the Texas coast from foreign intrusion. It was captured three times during the Mexican Independence movement: by Juan Bautista de las Casas in 1811; by José Bernardo de Gutiérrez and Augustus Magee in 1813; and by James Long in 1821. In 1835 it fell to Texas volunteers under George Collinsworth, and in 1836 it was renamed Fort Defiance by James W. Fannin. Fannin's defeat by José de Urrea actually occurred, not at the fort, but several miles away while he was trying to escape. Today, as skillfully and carefully restored, it presents the best example of Spanish presidial architecture in the United States.

La Bahía was the last Texas post to be inspected; Laredo, for which the party left on November 12, was under the jurisdiction of Nuevo Santander. Reaching it a week later, Lafora found it to be a dismal settlement of sixty huts on both sides of the Rio Grande. The settlers were armed and functioned as a volunteer guard under a militia captain for defense against Indians, but there was no presidio. The expedition did not tarry there, leaving the next morning for San Juan Bautista. The presidio there, which in earlier years had been the starting point for the settlement of Texas, was under the jurisdiction of Coahuila. From there the expedition worked south, inspecting the presidios on the route to Mexico City which they reached on February 23, 1768.

Rubí and Lafora had not been favorably impressed by anything they had seen. The mission system in Texas was, in their eyes, a dismal failure. The military system was a shambles: corruption among the officers, low morale among the troops, decaying and nonfunctioning arms and equipment, and crumbling, useless fortifications.

The first Texas troops they encountered had been the detachment from the San Sabá presidio temporarily stationed at San Lorenzo de la Santa Cruz. There were no fortifications there, and Lafora thought the site was poorly chosen for defense. The troops were quartered in mud *jacales*. At the San Sabá presidio itself, they found the garrison to be spooky to the point of paranoia about Indian attacks. There was indeed a menace from the hostiles but not in proportion to the fear that ran through the garrison. Apparently the stone walls of the fortress were in good enough condition at the time of the inspection, since there was no comment on them. But of the seven cannons, only three were serviceable, and these were mounted on carriages that were unsafe. Rubí recommended that all of the western posts be closed—the San Sabá presidio, the mission and garrison of El Cañon, and the Candelaria Mission.

Military conditions at San Antonio were deplorable. Aguayo, in 1721, had made the Bexar presidio there into a rather redoubtable fortress, garrisoned by one hundred men. The complement was twenty, plus a sergeant and a captain, when Rubí arrived. It can be inferred from later documents that the presidio was in a grave state of disrepair. The troops were not actually residing there, but were dispersed among the outlying missions. Lafora believed that the missions housed enough Indian warriors to protect themselves; the soldiers were thus uselessly engaged in unnecessary guard duty, while the presidio and villa of San Fernando lay unprotected. The horses belonging to the presidio were uncared for and many were regularly being stolen by marauding Indians.

Los Adaes, with its muster of sixty men and officers, was in little better shape. The log stockade walls were rotting into ruin and the buildings were unrepaired and decaying. Since the Indians of the region were not warlike and, after the 1763 transfer of Louisiana to Spain, no defense against the French was needed, the inspector recommended its abandonment. Orcoquisac was even in worse condition. Partially burned in the Pacheco debacle and never rebuilt, it too was virtually in ruins. Its location was unhealthy and almost inaccessible, in the midst of swamps and marshes. No nation, said Lafora, would ever attempt to colonize this place. It too should be abandoned. The La Bahía or Loreto presidio was the largest in Texas, well-built of stone and mortar, and garrisoned by a company of fifty. Although the climate was unhealthy, with few of the troops or civilians able to escape malaria and many dying of scurvy, the visitors found the La Bahía settlement to be the strongest in Texas at that time.

Rubí's findings may be summarized as follows:

I. El Cañon, including Candelaria: 4 priests, no neophytes (mission Indians), 30 soldiers, annual salaries (estimated) of 12,999 pesos, useless.

II. San Sabá: 100 soldiers, annual salaries of 40,360 pesos, useless.

III. San Antonio: 10 priests, 809 neophytes, 22 soldiers, annual salaries of 13,095 pesos.

IV. East Texas, including all three missions: 6 priests, no neophytes, 64 soldiers, annual salaries of 30,465 pesos, including the governor at 2,500 pesos, useless.

V. Orcoquisac: 2 priests, no neophytes, 31 soldiers, annual salaries of 13,245 pesos, useless.

VI. La Bahía, including two missions: 3 priests, 100 neophytes, 50 soldiers, annual salaries of 20,630 pesos.

On the basis of Rubí's report and recommendations, together with the keen observations of José de Gálvez, the Crown ultimately issued in 1772 an order that became a basic document of Southwestern frontier history: *Reglamento e instruccion para los presidios que se han de formar en la linea de frontera de la Nueva España,* commonly known as the "New Regulations." This royal order totally reformed and revamped the northern military frontier. It contained fourteen major revisionary articles plus specific orders for each presidio in the frontier cordon of posts.

Article One. Presidial captains were forbidden to buy supplies or sell supplies to their troops, and the office of paymaster was created to correct that evil.

Article Two. Fourteen presidios would be retained for the frontier cordon, each garrisoned by 47 troops including the officers, except Loreto at La Bahía which would have 55. San Antonio was the only other post to remain active in Texas, but it was not included in the line of fourteen and was to garrison 77 soldiers, a chaplain, 2 lieutenants, an ensign, and a captain who was to serve also as the governor of Texas. The salaries of all ranks were set, with the governor of Texas receiving an increase to 4,000 pesos annually.

Article Three. The uniform of the frontier soldier was to consist of a short blue woolen jacket with small cuffs and collar of red; blue wool breeches; a three-quarter length, sleeveless leather jacket of four to six thicknesses of hides for protection; a blue cloth cap and wide-brimmed black sombrero; shoes with leather leggings; a black cloth neckerchief; and a cartridge pouch and antelope skin bandoleer embroidered with the name of the presidio.

Article Four. Each soldier was to be issued a broad sword, lance, shield, musket, and pistols. Each company was to have an armorer to keep the weapons in good condition. Each soldier was also to have six horses, a colt, a mule, and a serviceable saddle.

Article Five. Each soldier was to receive in cash two *reales* every day, with the remainder of his salary, less deductions (one of which was 100 pesos withheld over a four to five year period for retirement purposes!), paid annually.

Article Six. Supplies for soldiers and their families would be ordered for them by the new paymaster, but merchants were not prohibited from entering the posts to trade directly with the soldiers.

Article Seven. Each soldier was to be issued three pounds of gunpowder a year. This was rarely fulfilled since powder and shot were invariably in short supply on the frontier.

Article Eight. A relatively intricate procedure was established to try to insure that promotions went to those who merited them.

Article Nine. Regular and accurate monthly strength reports were required of each post.

Article Ten. Indian prisoners were to be well treated, and presidio commanders were enjoined to seek peace treaties with any hostiles, except the Apaches, who could not be trusted.

Article Eleven. The presidios were to encourage adjacent civil settlement, and presidial captains were to assign land and lots to such settlers.

Article Twelve. A new administrative agency called the *Provincias Internas* (Interior Provinces) was created to expedite the governance of the frontier. This article outlined in detail the duties and responsibilities of the commandant of the Interior Provinces.

Article Thirteen. The duties and responsibilities of each rank were carefully defined.

Article Fourteen. The new position of paymaster was explained together with procedural details designed at the least to inhibit fiscal corruption in the presidios.

Military Cordon. In Texas, the presidios at Los Adaes, Orcoquisac, and San Sabá (together with the detachment at El Cañon) were to be closed. The presidio Loreto at La Bahía, the easternmost post in the cordon that stretched across the entire American Southwest, was to be retained, and the presidio Bexar at San Antonio was to be strengthened to over eighty men, the garrisons of Los Adaes and Orcoquisac being reassigned there. San Antonio was also designated the capital, with the governor to reside there and command the presidio.

MAP 2

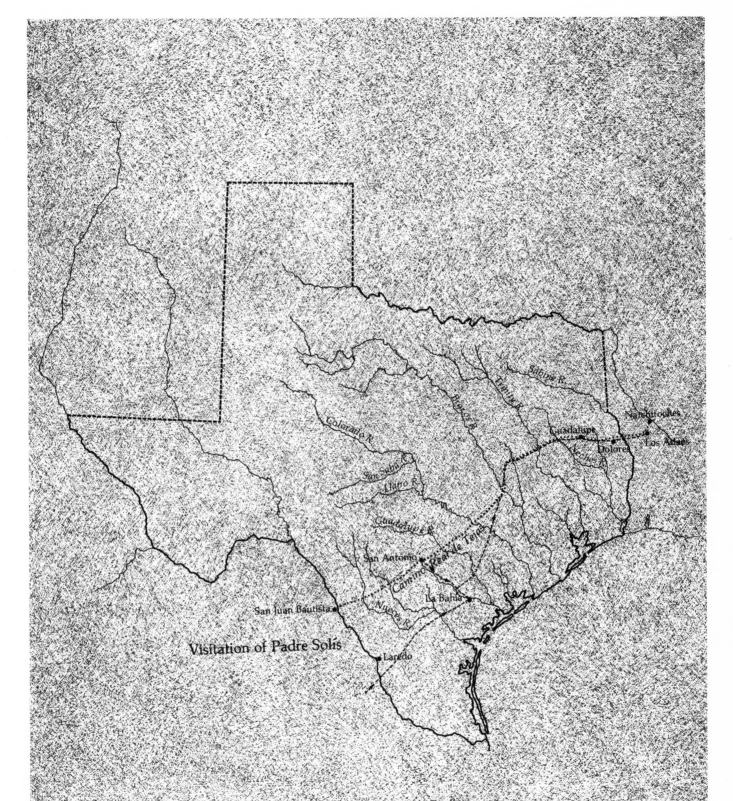

Visitation of Padre Solís

THE MISSIONS

3

The "Little Brothers of Assissi"—Franciscan friars in brown robes loosely tied with a knotted white cord—took vows of poverty when they entered the order. A masochistic interpretation by some held that poverty meant walking, not riding, and that shoes or boots were a luxury. So figuratively barefooted, but actually clad in sandals, the brown-robed monks trudged into Texas during the eighteenth century, and in the weary miles back and forth across the province, any tired or footsore padre who sneaked into a cart or climbed onto the back of a mule can be forgiven.

They came to Texas to bring Christianity to the heathen Indians, as they did throughout the Spanish colonial world. The padres built missions wherever they went, from *jacales* and crude, temporary thatched huts, to grand and glorious architectural monuments. The ideal and at least ostensible purpose of the missions and the padres was to Christianize the Indians, to save their souls, and to teach them the basic arts of civilization—cattle raising, farming, sewing, spinning, leatherwork, and such skills. Thus trained for useful life the erstwhile savage pagans would become loyal subjects of the Spanish Crown and good citizens of the empire. For generations to come they could then be exploited as workers for the large Spanish estates, bound to peonage in a system not far removed from Middle Age serfdom and not far different from outright slavery.

And that, the ultimate destiny of the Christianized Indian, reveals the practical and real, as opposed to the ideal and ostensible, purpose of the mission. In the Indians' native condition they were useless to the Spanish conquerors; as sullen and resentful slaves, they were little better; but as meek and docile "Christians," they would dutifully accept their role as exploited laborers—and the peculiar conscience of the Spaniard could glory in the salvation of the pagans. Although the conquerors were rarely candid, even to themselves, about the actual goal of the system, the common term for the native who had been programmed by the process, which in that age of the Inquisition was often quite forceful, was *indios reducidos,* for which the English cognate is obvious.

The mission system did not work well in Texas where most of the tribes were too savage to accept reduction gracefully, and but a few Indians ever accepted it at all. The warlike nomads of the plains, such as the Apaches and Comanches, were unconquerable; the agrarian woodland people, like the Caddoes, sullenly rejected the new god and the servile life style the padres tried to impose; and the South Texas Indians, from the Karankawas along the coast to the Coahuiltecans of the semiarid southwest region, were entirely too primitive. Consequently, the mission effort in Texas, judged either by its ideal or by its practical purpose, was a dismal failure. For the most part, those missions that did survive and endure into the nineteenth century did so because they were staffed at least in part by Indians imported from Mexico.

But, though the missions failed of their basic goals in Texas, they succeeded in quite another sense. Spain used them to stake out her claim to the Texas area and to prevent the French from occupying it. Thus, the abortive colony of Fort St. Louis, established by La Salle, provoked the first mission in Texas; when the French threat passed away, the mission was abandoned. The entrance of Louis de St. Denis on the Texas stage brought a response in a second mission wave: six missions and a presidio in East Texas and a mission and presidio as a supply station at San Antonio. The vague French threat imposed by the "Chicken War" of 1719 spurred the third wave of mission activity: reestablishment of the East Texas field; a new presidio at Los Adaes; and the mission and presidio of La Bahía at the site of Fort St. Louis, which were later moved twice to their final location at present Goliad. And, during the fourth period of expansion, the settlement was made at Orcoquisac because of rumors of French trading north of Galveston Bay. So the French were kept out of the Texas area, and colonial administrators could claim success, even if the system had produced few Christians and little native labor.

It is little wonder then that the ousting of the French from North America in 1763 and the transfer of Louisiana to Spain ended the need for mission support in Texas. So, just as the Marqués de Rubí had inspected the frontier military establishment to recommend readjustments, Father José de Solís was to visit the Texas missions. He did not accompany the *visitador*, but he toured the missions only a few months afterward, from February through May 1768.

Solís crossed the Rio Grande at the short-lived settlement of Dolores, in the northwest corner of present Zapata County about 25 to 30 miles below Laredo. At Dolores, which Solís referred to as a stock farm, he was met by a military escort from the presidio at San Antonio. His journal records that it took him from February 16 to February 26 to reach the Mission Rosario, or approximately twice as long as it required Rubí to travel the same distance. He found Rosario, which had been established thirteen years earlier, to be in good condition, although ministering to few Indians. Most, he recorded, had fled to the seashore or to the hills. Such a condition was typical for both Rosario and Espíritu Santo (La Bahía). The coastal Indians simply were not amenable to mission life; the Indians who were imported to operate the missions and to serve as examples frequently ran away to join their wilder brothers in the easy-going life of beachcombers. Out of curiosity, perhaps, a number of the wandering Indians returned to Rosario to see the visiting Father Solís.

Rosario was flourishing at the time of the visit. It possessed substantial livestock, including, in addition to small herds of asses, mules, and horses, some five thousand head of cattle, two hundred milk cows, and seven hundred sheep. A stout stockade surrounded the stone living quarters of both priests and Indians. The chapel, also of stone, was whitewashed on the exterior and plastered with clay inside. Solís found all of the required religious articles, such as sacred vessels, vestments, pulpit, confessional, and baptismal, to be clean, complete, and in their proper place in the church.

At the La Bahía mission, Espíritu Santo, he also found the holy articles in proper condition and deemed the mission generally to be in better shape than Rosario. Although the mission chapel was smaller than Rosario's, the other buildings, including the Indians' quarters, were large and respectable. Espíritu Santo owned almost twice as much livestock and had better farms because these could be irrigated from the river while those at Rosario could not because of the steep banks at its location. Solís reported that there were nearly three hundred Indians living at the missions, "but they have the same bad habits, inclinations, and vices" as the other Indians in Texas. Solís, it must be noted, was a prude with a sly interest in native sex life.

After spending nearly a month at these two missions (and the Loreto presidio across the river from Espíritu Santo), Solís left for San Antonio, passing several ranches on the route. His diary's description of the San Antonio settlement, with its five missions, presidio, and villa, is sadly very skimpy, except for his report on San José. Only it, of the five missions there, was under his jurisdiction. Texas had been missionized by Franciscans from both the *colegios* at Querétero and Zacatecas. These two houses had divided the evangelical activity in the province. Queréteran fathers had established three of the missions in the East Texas field, plus the Alamo at San Antonio; padres from Zacatecas had founded the other three in East Texas, plus La Bahía. The short-lived San Xavier missions on the San Gabriel had been Queréteran as were the two on the upper Nueces at El Cañon. Zacatecans were responsible for San José and Rosario (and much later, Refugio). Following an inspection by Pedro de Rivera, the three Queréteran missions had moved to San Antonio. Thus, at the time of Solís' visit there, only San José was operated by the *colegio* at Zacatecas. The reverend visitor was as much impressed by Mission San José y San Miguel de Aguayo in 1768 as anyone is today who visits the gracefully lovely structures that constitute the restored mission, now a National Historic Site.

San José maintained a very substantial irrigated farm of over four thousand acres which was the primary source of food supply for all of the Zacatecan missions in Texas. Here were grown corn, beans, lentils, melons, peaches, potatoes, sugar cane, and many varieties of vegetables. About 30 miles to the south the mission maintained a ranch, known as El Atascoso, which was a rather big operation.

Numerous asses and breeding mares were kept there for the production of mules, as well as 1,500 yoke of oxen and 5,000 head of sheep.

Leaving San José during a freezing, wet norther, Father Solís fell in with a caravan of some 100 travelers who were on their way to Los Adaes. As Rubí had done, they moved southeast to the Guadalupe River near present Cuero and then turned northeast toward East Texas. Solís' diary is more descriptive of Texas in its natural state than most of the other Spanish documents. On this journey from San Antonio to Los Adaes he commented frequently on both the abundance and variety of wild game: deer, bear, bison, beaver, otter, and wild Castillian horses and cattle which had multiplied from pairs left near the Colorado for that purpose by Alonso de León in 1690. Birds of all kinds were everywhere to be seen. Solís especially noted the large quantity of wild turkeys and quail. Any one of the rivers he crossed would have been a fisherman's paradise, although there were snakes and occasional alligators. He described a native breed of dog with a very thin, pointed nose that he thought was a cross between a wolf and a coyote. Domesticated by the Tejas Indians, it was "just as dishonest as its masters."

Solís visited the three East Texas missions of Guadalupe, Dolores, and San Miguel and was only a little better impressed with them than Rubí and Lafora had been. The Guadalupe mission at present Nacogdoches had an adobe chapel surrounded by a wooden railing, as was the priests' house, which he described as a fine frame building, although it was unquestionably a log house. There were several buildings, also presumably of logs, that housed soldiers, a kitchen, and a granary. "At some distance there are other good houses, all of which are roomy and respectable," he wrote, but did not describe their purpose. The priests there maintained some livestock and tilled a small farm. He reported no neophytes at the mission and only twelve baptisms on the records—a paltry score for evangelical work of fifty years at the site.

There were only eleven baptisms recorded at Nuestra Señora de los Dolores de los Ais. The wood church was neat and clean, as were the dwelling quarters. There were apparently no other structures. Solís found the mission poor in temporal goods, its small herds frequently robbed by the Ais Indians and the priests occasionally suffering minor deprivations. Said Solís: "The Indians of the Ais tribe are the worst in the province. They are addicted to drunkenness, dishonesty, *mitotes* and other dances, and to every kind of vice, especially lust." The visitor believed that the priests there were in some peril, for the Indians scoffed them and had on occasion "gone so far as to lay their hands on them."

The settlement at Los Adaes was located on a small plain with a low hill on each side of it. The presidio (Linares) was on one of these hills, and the mission (San Miguel) stood on the other. As Rubí had found the presidio stockade rotting, so Solís found the mission buildings literally falling to ruin. The sacred articles of the mission were uncared for, and the mission had "deteriorated both materially and spiritually." No Indians were at the mission, although the records listed 103 baptisms. There were no crops raised and apparently no livestock. There was a scarcity of everything except wine, which was supplied by the nearby French at Natchitoches. The padres at the mission did serve the ministerial needs of the soldiers at the presidio and the settlers in the vicinity.

Although Solís did not report on any of the Queréteran missions, or even visit Orcoquisac or El Cañon, it is apparent from Rubí's casual observations that all of the missions in Texas were suffering a malaise which varied only in degree. They were unable to "reduce" very many Indians to Christinity.

There was no common or universal reason for the failure of the missions to fulfill their primary (nominal) or secondary (practical) objectives, except that the Indians in Texas were not amenable to reduction. In the west, the plains tribes, especially the Apache, were nomadic hunters to whom a sedentary mission life was unacceptable. Additionally, their way of life and the cultural patterns developed over generations put emphasis on qualities that denied the state of peonage required by the ultimate surrender to the padres. In short, they were too fierce, too hostile, and too individualistic. The coastal bands, such as the Karankawa, were too primitive and too wild. Their culture had developed even less in the way of institutional patterns than the plains folk. Indeed, they were virtually anarchical in terms of social organization. Among cultures lacking institutionalism or much social organization, the padres had to do much more than simply switch the people from their native ways to the Spanish way. The mission fathers, who had enjoyed considerable success with sedentary Indian tribes in central Mexico, never really understood that it was far more difficult to impose social structure on a disorganized people than it was to replace gradually the institutions that existed. The Indians of the East Texas woodlands, on the other hand, were a highly organized and institutionalized people. They were also sedentary and agrarian. It is possible that a stronger effort might have brought them into the missions. However, it might not have, for Caddoan society was complex and vital, and those Indians had a strong belief in their own religion as well as a strong sense of individualism.

One generalization can be made. The missions had little to offer any of the Texas Indian groups that contributed positively to their lives. The Indians had developed viably successful economics based on their own environment. The western hunters could usually find game; the beachcombers of the coast already knew how to fish and to scavenge the flotsam and jetsam; and the Caddoan farmers were already competent agriculturists. They gratefully accepted from the padres presents of European tools and weapons, of course. And in times of draught or poor hunting, some Indians would even move into the mission temporarily to feed off of Spanish supplies. Winter, for instance, often brought an upturn in the mission populations. But with the coming of spring, away they would go—to fish or to hunt or to plant their own crops. The padres' inducements then became insufficiently attractive, and Texas was too vast and too open to make the use of force practical. Since mission life, for the Indians, was essentially a trade of freedom for security, desertion was a serious problem for the padres. Indians would come in, stay a few months or even a year or so, but most would ultimately leave. Too, the Indians may have recognized that the security of the mission was often illusionary, for European diseases frequently spread like wildfire through the close-packed Indian quarters in the missions.

So, after a half-century of effort, there were no Indians (Lipan Apaches) in the two missions on the Nueces; the mission on the San Saba had been destroyed and never rebuilt; the three missions on the San Gabriel (for the Tonkawas) had been abandoned; there were no neophytes and only a handful of baptismal records in the three East Texas missions (primarily for Caddoan peoples); neither Bidais nor Orcoquisas lived at the Orcoquisac mission; Espíritu Santo and Rosario together could not hold the Karankawas who frequently even tempted imported Indians away; and the five missions at San Antonio shared an unstable Indian population (mostly primitive Coahuiltecan bands) of around eight hundred, counting as Solís said "big and little of both sexes."

Even if the church had been powerful and determined in Texas, some reorganization was almost inevitable. However, in 1767 a cataclysm shook every part of the religious community and made mission reorganization mandatory. The Jesuits were expelled! There were many Jesuit missions in New Spain (although none had been established in Texas), and the Franciscans had to take over their operation. This task fell to the older of the Franciscan houses, the *colegio* at Querétero. This sudden demand on its resources spread them too thinly. And thus it was that the Queréteran missions in Texas were transferred to the mother house at Zacatecas in 1772.

This transfer was coincident with the promulgation of the "New Regulations," and the Zacatecan fathers tailored their reorganization in Texas to the changes Rubí had recommended. The Queréteran missions at Orcoquisac and El Cañon were simply closed. The four Queréteran missions at San Antonio were transferred to the jurisdiction of Zacatecas. In the Spanish bureaucratic tradition, careful inventories of the four properties and the articles within them were made, some of which are extant today in the research library at San José Mission. The three Zacatecan missions in East Texas were quietly abandoned. It is particulary worth noting in connection with the Guadalupe Mission at Nacogdoches that the padres apparently gathered up the vestments and religious articles, closed the doors, and walked out, leaving behind a number of log buildings, including the church, in usable if not excellent condition. It was these buildings that became a few years later the nucleus of a new civil settlement in Texas.

MAP 3

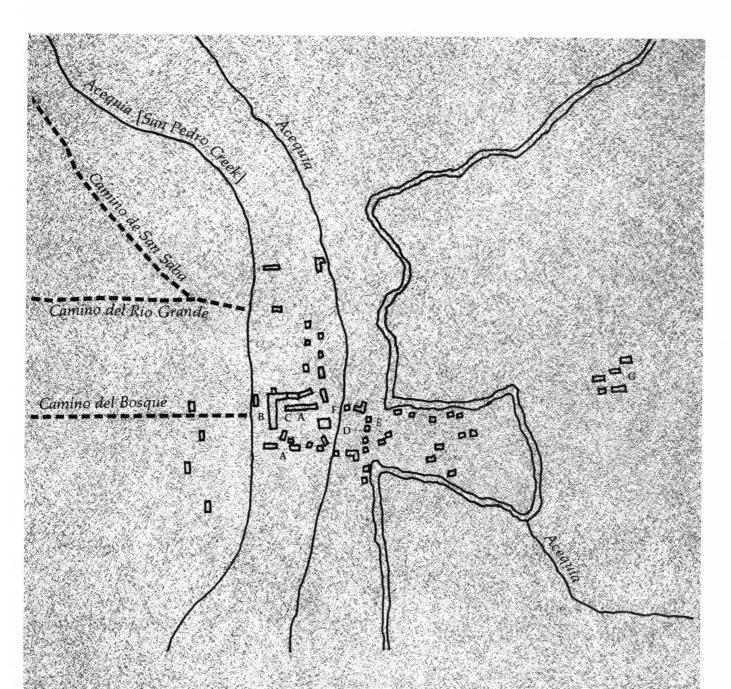

Acequia [San Pedro Creek]

Acequia

Camino de San Saba

Camino del Rio Grande

Camino del Bosque

B

C A

F

D

E

A

G

Acequia

San Antonio as rendered by Lafora 1767
[on modern base]

A. Presidio
B. Captain's quarters
C. Guard house
D. Plaza
E. Official buildings
F. Church
G. Mission

THE REFUGEES

4

Los Adaes was the dying capital of Texas at the time of the official visitations of the Marqués de Rubí, Nicolás de Lafora, and Father José de Solís. The presidio palisade was rotting, the mission was useless, and the previous governor and captain of the presidio, Angel de Martos y Navarrete was a disgrace to the Spanish Crown. He had lived like an Indian, dressed like a peon, and was said to have made many pesetas in illegal trade with both the French and the Indians. He was removed from office and brought to trial, ostensibly for his responsibility for burning the presidio of Orcoquisac. His replacement, on a temporary basis, was red-haired Hugo Oconor, one of a number of Irish Catholics who had fled British persecution at home to seek a new life in the service of Catholic Spain on the frontier.

It was clear to Oconor that Los Adaes and the entire East Texas establishment, including Orcoquisac, would be abandoned. As both Rubí and Solís had pointed out, four useless missions and two worthless presidios were a needless drain on the royal treasury. And the Spanish acquisition of Louisiana took away any value that the continued maintenance of a post in East Texas might have had. Yet the *ad interim* governor had no orders to close the posts, so they lingered in waning evanescence for nearly a half-dozen years longer. Presumably life at the missions and at Los Adaes changed little if any from what it had been in 1767. Oconor visited Los Adaes and was there at the time of Rubí's inspection, but unlike Martos he did not take up residence at the presidio.

Though the death knell of East Texas was being rung in official minds, apparently the settlers in the region had no forebodings of the impending doom. They continued ranching, farming, and trading with the Indians as they had done for nearly half a century. Many of the families living on the farmsteads that were scattered between the Mission Guadalupe at present Nacogdoches and Los Adaes were into the second and in some instances possibly the third generation in Texas. To them the region was home. There they felt secure, and few would have any remorse if the soldiers were withdrawn or the priests transferred. That they, too, would be ordered to leave their fields and their farms apparently never occurred to them. There is some evidence that the number of civilians in East Texas increased between 1767 and 1773. One historian has suggested that French settlers from Louisiana may have shifted into the region. But the strengthening of East Texas, even by civil occupation alone, was not on the colonial drawing board.

A new governor was appointed for Texas in 1769. The Baron Juan María Vicencio de Ripperdá was from a Spanish ducal line of great prominence. Shortly after reaching Mexico he married an aristocratic lady from Guadalajara. Ripperdá and his bride took up residence in San Antonio in 1770—yet another sign of the demise of Los Adaes. Other governors before him had lived in San Antonio, but none since Manuel de Sandoval had officially been in residence there. Sandoval was arrested in 1737 for not staying in the capital of Los Adaes. The past governors of Texas had also served as the captains of the presidial garrison at Los Adaes. Nonetheless part of the structure in San Antonio today grandly known as the "Royal Governor's Palace" was apparently built prior to 1750. A lintel over the entrance is carved with the date of 1749. Ripperdá may have made, and it seems reasonable that he would have, extensive modifications to the building. However, his successor, Domingo Cabello, in 1778 found the building in such bad repair that he occupied the jail for temporary quarters.

Whatever Baron Ripperdá did about construction of his official residence, shortly after his arrival, he did establish a new military post a few miles east of San Antonio in 1771. Located where the road to La Bahía crossed Cibolo Creek, it was named Santa Cruz del Cíbolo but was commonly called Arroyo del Cíbolo. Nothing remains of the post today.

In 1773 Ripperdá received orders from Hugo Oconor to implement the "New Regulations" and specifically to evacuate the civilian settlers in the East Texas area. Oconor had been promoted to a new position created by the "New Regulations," that of Inspector (inspector comandante) of the Interior Provinces. Oconor's orders amplified the "New Regulations," requiring Ripperdá to go personally to East Texas and supervise the removal of the population to San Antonio. Oconor probably sensed that there would be resistance to the move, and, as a matter of fact, Ripperdá himself was not sympathetic toward the order.

Nevertheless, he left promptly on his unhappy errand. Since Orcoquisac had already been evacuated, he did not go there. The padres in the other three missions, Guadalupe (Nacogdoche), Dolores (Ais) and Pilar (Adaes), had received notification from Zacatecas and were eager to leave. Ripperdá took possession of the ornaments that had been furnished the missions by the Crown, and the padres packed up the religious articles to be carried to the colegio at Zacatecas. It is worth noting that the padres simply vacated the mission buildings. At Guadalupe where the structures were in a good state of repair, they were left standing empty and abandoned.

Ripperdá reported that he was met at the Guadalupe Mission by a large number of Tejas Indians who begged him not to abandon the area. The governor cynically but correctly thought that the Indians would miss the presents and the illicit trade. He also thought that the Tejas feared attacks from Lipan Apaches and wanted the protection of Spanish soldiers, but this was probably unlikely. In the first place, the area was much too far east for attacks from Plains Indians, and in the second place, it is doubtful that the Tejas had much respect for the handful of soldiers who had been garrisoned near the mission over the years.

At Los Adaes, where he arrived on June 6 after a journey of eight days, he ordered that everyone, soldiers and civilians alike, must be ready to march for Bexar on June 11. Five days! It was a savagely short notice for such an abrupt and traumatic upheaval, and it must have caused panic and chaos. At that time of the year most of the settlers had crops growing in their fields, perhaps with some corn nearly ready to be harvested. Many families found themselves being preemptorily ordered out of homes where they had lived for years—some for over a generation. They pleaded with Ripperdá for more time, and he granted a brief extension. But perhaps his initial five-day notice was the best way for him to execute the cruel order, as it would have gotten the settlers on the move while they were still in a state of shock. The delay enabled some to flee to the woods and others to organize themselves to circumvent the move.

The governor left for San Antonio on June 14. One lieutenant, José Gonzales who had served for 40 years at Los Adaes and must have been in his sixties, was left in command to oversee the evacuation. It was a miserable affair. They had to leave by June 25. That barely gave them time enough to gather their livestock, load up their household goods, and pack their personal belongings. Much of the livestock was too scattered to be collected. Inadequate supplies for the long journey were packed. There were not enough wagons and carts, and one can imagine the frenetic effort to repair them. In the hasty loading, some treasured household item may, here or there, have taken the place of supplies for the journey. Aging Gonzales' effectiveness as a leader for this exodus might also be questioned. It was said that when the day came to leave he rode from house to house driving the people out of their homes. A later report stated that thirty-five people from Los Adaes took refuge in the forest rather than face this forced eviction.

The clumsy, reluctant entourage nonetheless moved out toward the Dolores mission at the old Ais Indian village. Approximately fifteen miles before they reached it they stopped at a rancho called El Lobanillo which must have been a fairly good-sized settlement. It was the home of a prominent citizen named Antonio Gil Ybarbo who soon would become the leader of these outcasts. Because of the interchangeability of letters in eighteenth century Spanish, the name has been rendered in a variety of ways—Ivarva, Ibarba, Yvarvo, etc. There is a strong suggestion that it may in fact have been Gil y Barvo. Father Solís referred to the rancho as Lobanillo de Gil in 1768.

Its proprietor was a native of Los Adaes, a second generation Texan then about forty years old. He was a trader who had already been dealing illegally with both the French (prior to 1763) and the Indians. At least once he had been arrested for this activity, which was customarily ignored by the officials. It would be assumed, therefore, that he had become a rather notorious operator. He was imprisoned for several months on the accusation that he had bought horses and mules from some Indians, which had been stolen from presidial remudas at San Antonio and San Sabá, and had sold them at Natchitoches and New Orleans. One report, made some years later by a man who was attempting to secure Ybarbo's dismissal from office, indicated that he was a mulatto, but given the time and circumstances, it does not seem likely that a mulatto would have emerged as the leader of the East Texans.

At the Lobanillo rancho, several people fell sick or feigned it and were allowed to drop out of the march and remain behind. In all, with those left to care for the sick, two dozen people were left behind. Included in those were Ybarbo's mother, his sister, and his sister-in-law. Was his mother left because he intended even then to return? Or did he strive so hard to return because he had left her at Lobanillo?

After some delay, the caravan moved on. At nearby Dolores the two priests and several citizens joined the motley company. But at Guadalupe, though the priests fell in readily enough, nine more people dropped out. There, Lt. Gonzales and two women died, perhaps of the rigors of the trip. The worst was yet to come. Under the nominal command of a sergeant, but now actually led by Ybarbo, the group started the long, long trek toward San Antonio. They left Guadalupe about the first of August and did not reach San Antonio until September 26. Ten children died on the road, and there was much suffering and privation. Many were forced to walk because of the shortage of riding animals. Heat, incessant rain, and flooded river crossings brought sickness to people and livestock. And, ill-provisioned from the start, they frequently went hungry when game could not be found. Twenty or thirty people, when the caravan reached Santa Cruz del Cíbolo, refused to budge farther. Within a few months after the emigrants finally reached San Antonio, another thirty people died, their health apparently destroyed by the arduous trip.

Almost immediately after their arrival in San Antonio, Governor Ripperdá told them that they were free to select town lots in the villa of San Fernando at no cost and that they would also be given pasturage outside the villa. To the "Adaesaños" who had stopped at the new post on the Cíbolo, he made a similar offer there if they preferred it to San Fernando. Instead of accepting land in either place, the refugees drew up a petition requesting that they be permitted to return to East Texas. Obviously, such a petition had been brewing among them during the weeks they had been on the trail.

The petition stated that the San Antonio area (San Fernando particularly) was too crowded, that if they settled there they would be infringing on the rights of others, that they were bankrupt and could not afford to make the necessary improvements, including the construction of a new *acequia*, that if they went back to East Texas they could recover much of their livestock, and that they wanted to establish a new settlement at the Dolores (Ais) Mission. This was of course near Ybarbo's home at Lobanillo. The document was signed by seventy-five men representing families totalling over two hundred people, a majority, it was said, of the East Texans who had reached San Antonio. An earlier estimate had put the East Texas population at five hundred.

Ripperdá favored the request of the exiles and wrote letters to the viceroy and to Oconor supporting the petition. In January 1774 Ybarbo, accompanied by one Gil Flores, left San Antonio to carry the petition to Viceroy Antonio María Bucareli y Ursua in Mexico City. Somewhat surprisingly they got prompt attention from the viceroy who at first acceded tentatively to the request. There may have been a matter of politics involved in the viceroy's ready support. Hugo Oconor opposed the resettlement of East Texas. The viceroy's initial approval inferred that the Adaesaños did not need Oconor's authorization but could act directly on the viceroy's authority. It does not seem illogical that the viceroy resented the special position that Oconor occupied as Inspector of the newly established Interior Provinces.

However, Oconor's objections stemmed from the fact that he believed the East Texans wanted to return to their old haunts primarily so that they could resume the profitable contraband Indian trade. His demurral in writing forced the viceroy to back down, but he did give a vague and ambiguous approval to Ybarbo's plan, equivocating on the one hand that anything the Adaesaños did must meet with Oconor's approval and on the other that permission must come from Ripperdá. He added additional confusion by writing to Ripperdá that under no circumstances was Ybarbo and his flock to be allowed to resettle around Natchitoches and by telling Ybarbo that any new settlement must be at least one hundred leagues (or about 265 miles) away from Natchitoches.

Ybarbo and Flores returned to San Antonio in the spring, and by the end of the summer had organized most of the East Texans for the venture of establishing a new pueblo within the vague parameters of the viceroy's permission. Ripperdá, who consistently seems to have supported them, authorized a settlement at a point where the road to Nacogdoches crossed the Trinity River. He placed Gil Ybarbo in charge and named Gil Flores his lieutenant. Oconor was later to complain that this location was even better suited for illicit trade than the old East Texas location. Some suspicion exists that Baron Ripperdá's support of Ybarbo derived from the governor's own personal involvement in contraband Indian trade. And of course Ybarbo himself had unquestionably been involved in this kind of nefarious work. On balance, it must be assumed that this was the underlying motive for the new settlement, which otherwise makes no sense at all. It is hopelessly illogical that the refugees from East Texas, who had pleaded so piteously to be allowed to return to their homes, would be willing and indeed eager to leave the settled area around San Antonio to go only part of the way back and build a new town in the wilderness.

But that is exactly what they did. The "little band of ignorant, poverty-stricken colonists," as Herbert E. Bolton described them, left San Antonio some time in August 1774. There were about seventy full-grown men and their families in the colonizing party; the remainder of the refugees planned to join them later. The governor sent some soldiers along to afford them protection, but not a priest although Ybarbo had requested one. Shortly after arriving at the Trinity crossing, Ybarbo took a small party to Los Adaes to gather nails, hinges, and other usable building materials, together with powder, shot, six cannons, and cannon carriages. He apparently at that time went into Natchitoches and apprised an old contact of his, Nicholas de la Mathe, a French trader, of the return of the Adaesaños to the Trinity —and to business. Another party struggled through the swamps and thickets to the deserted Orcoquisac presidio and brought back two cannons as well as other building supplies.

The new town was given a name that incorporated the memory of Los Adaes with recognition of the viceroy: Nuestra Señora del Pilar de Bucareli. It was commonly called Bucareli. It was laid out with the buildings forming a rectangular plaza, according to both law and tradition. The buildings were of log and wattle construction. A stockade was built to enclose the village for protection. A small chapel at one end of the plaza was furnished with some of the ornaments that had been removed from East Texas by the governor. A year after its founding, Bucareli consisted of twenty good houses of hewn timber, the church, a guardhouse, and a number of *jacales.*

Two years later, in 1777, there were fifty hewn timber houses and a new church. The river crossing had been improved, fields opened, ranchos established, and corrals built. The population was reported at 125 men, 87 women, 128 children, and 5 slaves. In the meantime, seventeen deaths had been reported, including that of Lt. Gil Flores, for which an undefined epidemic was blamed. The new church building was donated by the Natchitoches trader Nicholas de la Mathe who visited the settlement in 1776 and then sent two carpenters to construct the chapel. A priest was sent from San Antonio some time in 1776. Apparently there were other visitors—traders—from Natchitoches from time to time.

Ybarbo began to have visions of a settlement more prosperous than Los Adaes had been. He encouraged the Bidai Indians of the vicinity to camp around Bucareli. He asked that a mission be built and a padre be sent to minister to the Indians, but nothing came of this scheme. He sent for cotton seed, wheat seed, sheep, and other agricultural supplies. He brought in a weaver to produce blankets and coarse cloth.

Nothing entered the records regarding contraband Indian trade, but Ybarbo, with the encouragement of the governor, made numerous visits to Indian bands to the north and to the east. The ostensible purpose of the visits—and certainly a valid one in itself—was to secure the friendship and allegiance of the Indians. Yet the circumstantial evidence was strong that illicit trade in contraband goods was a mainstay of the community's economy. Hugo Oconor remained suspicious of the Adaesaños. One of his men, Captain Luis Cazorla, reported that "it appears that the sole motive of the subjects who go to Bucareli to live is to smuggle and be free of the yoke of justice." Oconor requested more than once that Bucareli be disbanded, as did the viceroy's *fiscal* who had advised against the settlement in 1774.

Another open purpose of Ybarbo's travels among the Indians was to search for the activities of English traders whose presence along the coast had been rumored by the Indians. To this there was some truth. In 1777 Ybarbo located a stranded English ship in Sabine Lake, but no Englishmen. The Orcoquisa Indians told him that the ship had entered that confluence of the Neches and Sabine earlier that spring, and that after it was run aground the crew had left overland promising to return. The Indians also said that another ship had come in two years earlier. On his return to Bucareli, Ybarbo found a naked Englishman named Miller ("Bautista Miler") who claimed to have been cast adrift in a canoe seven months earlier by an unscrupulous captain named Joseph David. Miller was taken to Bucareli; no further record of him has survived. Nor were there any more reports of wandering Englishmen or English vessels.

The prosperity of Bucareli was short-lived. In May 1778 a band of thirty Comanches rode up to the village. The appearance of these dreaded Indians raised an alarm out of all proportion to their small number. Ybarbo and his militia chased the Comanches off, overtook them near the Brazos, and killed at least three. There may not have been a connection between this first Comanche encounter and the second one, six months later, in October 1778. With a much larger party they swooped down and drove off nearly three hundred horses. The militia followed them but did not attack and did not recover the plunder.

Rumors began to build up that the Comanches planned to destroy Bucareli, burning its wooden buildings and carrying the women into captivity. Fear approaching the dimensions of hysteria pervaded the Spaniards. The priest wrote that the inhabitants were afraid to leave the stockade to care for their fields or livestock and that they feared even to go out to hunt except in large parties. They mounted a twenty-four hour guard over their horse herds and in the village. And this preoccupation with defense left them no time to work at sustaining the settlement. They began to talk of moving farther east and even requested permission to do so. They also begged for military aid. But neither relief nor permission to move was forthcoming.

In January 1779, entirely without official sanction, the Adaesaños began their return to East Texas. Captain Ybarbo remained at Bucareli with a guard of about twenty men while the majority of the families with as much of their goods as they could cart started up the old trail to the former Guadalupe Mission. The plan was that when they reached Guadalupe they would send back for the remainder of their goods and livestock and the rest of the families. Before they could do so Bucareli was destroyed in a double tragedy, and Ybarbo and his men scurried after the settlers.

It was on the night of February 14 that this final disaster fell. The Trinity River, swollen by flood, broke out of its banks and virtually inundated the village. The people and some of the livestock were saved on hastily thrown together rafts. They pitched camp on high ground away from the river. A few nights later Comanches struck and ran off with most of the remaining horses. At some point, either before or after the Comanche raid, about half the houses burned. Using their improvised boats, the remaining villagers crossed the Trinity. The next night there was either another Indian attack or a threat of one, which was equally frightening. In fright and despair, they headed northeast to join the others.

Thus, some time in March or April 1779, they regrouped at the Mission Guadalupe. The buildings there, evacuated six years earlier, were apparently still in reasonably good condition. From that time hence the settlement was called Nacogdoches, as indeed it had frequently been referred to earlier. And from that time also it has remained a permanent town in Texas. Although it had been founded without official authorization, it soon received tacit recognition and later full approval.

MAP 4

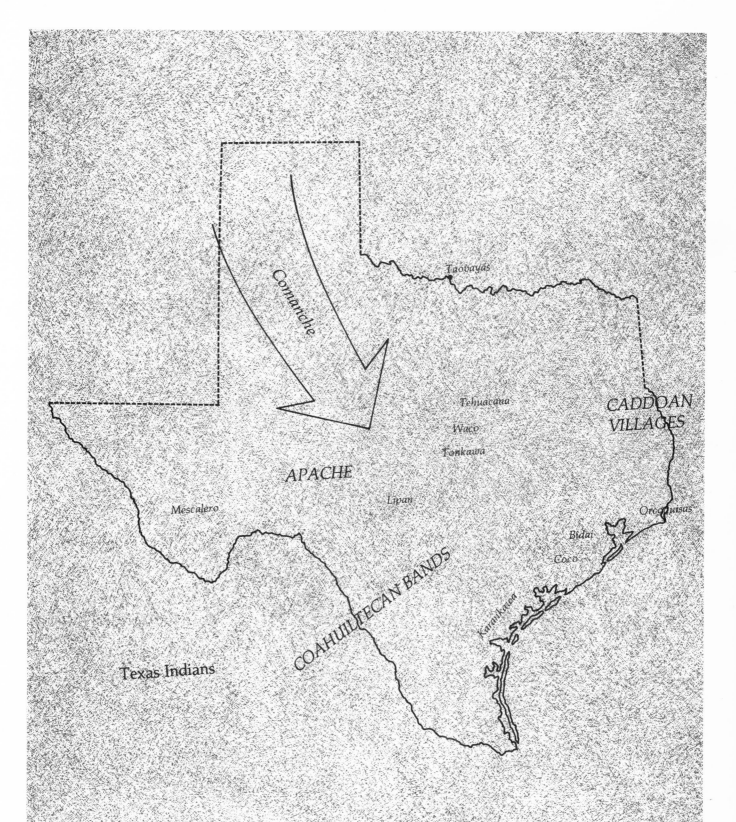

Taobayas

Tehuacana

Waco

Tonkawa

CADDOAN
VILLAGES

Comanche

APACHE

Mescalero

Lipan

Orcoquisas

Bidai

Coco

COAHUILTECAN BANDS

Karankawa

Texas Indians

THE INDIANS

5

Over thousands of years and through unnumbered generations humankind developed an agrarian society in the humid eastern part of Texas and a nomadic hunting society in the semiarid western reaches of the state. Archeologists use a cultural level classification to describe early man in Texas. The first, called Paleo-American, represents Stone Age hunters of a very primitive level of development. The second, Archaic, represents the beginnings of agriculture and the development of weapons and hunting techniques. In the third stage Neo-Americans became clearly differentiated by the climate: sedentary agricultural villages in East Texas; relatively sophisticated bands of hunters in West Texas.

By the seventeenth century, the Caddoan Indians of the piney woods were far and away the most culturally developed people in the state's area. The Jumanos of the Big Bend, also clearly into the Neo-American stage, represented the most advanced nomadic society in West Texas. At that period, the beginning of more than casual exploratory Spanish contact, most of the remainder of the Indian bands were in some phase of Archiac stage development. A few were apparently scarcely above the Paleo-American levels. Among these most primitive of peoples were the numerous little bands referred to—for want of a better name—as Coahuiltecans. The coastal bands, even several generations later than Cabeza de Vaca's visit, remained at a low level of Archaic development.

The later part of the seventeenth century witnessed a major change in the western Indians. A more advanced hunting people, mounted on horses pilfered from Spanish herds, swooped across the Texas plains. These were the Apaches, fiercer and more war-like than any of the miscellaneous bands that roamed the area, and even the Jumanos, who may have been culturally as advanced, were no match for them in battle. By the turn of the century the Apaches, in two major tribal groups—Lipan and Mescalero—dominated all of West Texas. At that time Wichita-speaking people, such as the Tehuacanoes and the Tonkawas, lived on the fringes of the plains and the prairies and in the Cross Timbers. In villages along the upper Red River an important tribe known as the Taovayas carried on trade and commerce with many of the Indian bands as well as with the French from Louisiana. Linguistically Wichita, their characteristics were such that some anthropologists have speculated whether the Taovayas were descended from the Jumanos.

The western regions of the Texas Indian cosmos changed again with the arrival from the north of a people even more hostile than the Apaches. These were a Shoshone-speaking people whose name was rendered phonetically into Spanish as Comanche. These implacable warriors conquered the Texas Plains during the eighteenth century, ultimately splitting the Lipan and Mescalero Apaches and driving on into northern Mexico on regular raids. Both Apaches and Comanches were by that time totally horse-borne cultures. They were skilled huntsmen, and their ways of life were primarily based on the vast buffalo herds that grazed the western plains and prairies. Neither people had any concept of territorial jurisdiction or land ownership; neither had any overall tribal organization; and neither was ever to be converted into mission Indian or agrarian villager. One would have thought that during the eighteenth century there would have been enough land and enough buffalo to maintain both Athapaskan-Apaches and Shoshone-Comanches, who together only numbered a few thousand. And indeed there was, but possibly because of their similarities, the two became irreconcilable foes.

The results of this enmity were first noted by the inspector Pedro de Rivera in 1728 who reported on the increase in Apache raids in Texas and northern Mexico. Not knowing that these Apache incursions resulted from Comanche pressures, General Rivera recommended a war of extinction against the Apaches. Had Rivera perceived the true cause of Apache depredation and had Spaniard joined with Apache against the early waves of Comanche invasion, they might just possibly have turned the Comanches back north from Texas. But by the time the Spaniards became fully aware of the Comanche presence, those dreadful hostiles were in control of the South Plains. Spanish Indian policy in the west of Texas (and northern Mexico and eastern New Mexico) thereafter vacillated between futile attempts to fight the Apaches and equally futile attempts to missionize them.

Thus, the mid-eighteenth century mission on the San Saba was established to befriend the Apaches in a reversal of Rivera's suggestion. The mission was lost in massacre and fire three years later when Spaniards got their first taste of Comanche vengeance. The two little missions on the upper Nueces which Rubí had viewed so disgustingly were founded in the aftermath, also to befriend the Apaches. Rubí, unlike Rivera, recognized the nature of the dilemma on the frontier: two mighty Indian hostiles, and Spain must choose between one or the other—must ally with one and war with the other. It only made good sense to Rubí that Spain should make alliances with the Comanches who were clearly the more powerful. With the formation of the unified frontier military administration known as the *Provencias Internas* or Interior Provinces, this became the foundation stone of Spanish Indian policy in the plains region.

The creation of the *Provencias Internas* emerged from the recommendations of the Marqués de Rubí and of José de Gálvez. The "New Regulations for Presidios" provided for the posts of commandant and inspector. Hugo Oconor, replaced as governor of Texas by Ripperdá, after a brief leave of absence in Mexico City and possibly an Indian campaign on the frontier, was promoted in rank and given the post of inspector. His command of the frontier actually preceded by a few months the establishment of the *Procencias Internas*. Oconor reached Chihuahua in December 1771 and in January replaced Bernardo de Gálvez, nephew of José de Gálvez, as the military commandant. Thus, although he did not hold the office of commander, Oconor was the organizing officer of the new administrative unit. It was his duty to relocate the cordon of presidios and to reorganize the frontier military forces according to the 1772 Regulations. During the four years in which he carried out this assignment he (and the frontier provinces) were under the jurisdiction of the viceroy. Finally, in 1776, the post of Commandant General of the Interior Provinces was filled, and the frontier provinces were sheared from the viceroy's direct control.

The new commander, no more Spanish than Dublin-born Oconor, was Teodoro de Croix of Lille, France. Of aristocratic lineage, De Croix was commissioned a junior officer in the Spanish army in 1747 at the age of seventeen. In 1765 he accompanied an uncle, the Marqués de Croix who served briefly as viceroy of New Spain, to Mexico. Serving with distinction in several posts in the New World, he rose to the rank of brigadier general. He had been in Spain at the time of his apointment and did not reach Mexico again until December 1776. There he found the viceroy somewhat less than cooperative because of a not unnatural resentment of the new quasi-independent military unit. De Croix immediately set about studying reports, assessing the situation on the frontier, and planning an inspection tour. José de Rubí replaced Oconor as inspector, the Irishman being promoted to brigadier and given command in Yucatan. Antonio de Bonilla, whose *Brief Compendium of the History of Texas* has been an important source of information about Spanish Texas for two hundred years, was named as secretary of the Interior Provinces. De Croix made other staff appointments as well as replaced a number of the presidial commanders under his now nearly autonomous jurisdiction. Finally, in August 1777, De Croix set out to visit the frontier states. With him, by his express wish, was Father Juan Agustín Morfí as chaplain. Morfí, after his return, compiled the first serious history of Texas. There were actually two distinct manuscripts: one, Memorias para la historia de Texas . . .; the other, Historia de Texas, 1673-1779. The latter was translated by Carlos Castañeda and published by the Quivera Society in 1935. Both of Morfí's literary-historical efforts were prompted apparently by his objections to Bonilla's *Breve Compendio.* Bonilla, also, accompanied De Croix on the inspection of the frontier, but there exists no record of animosity arising between the secretary and the chaplain while on the eight-month expedition.

De Croix was primarily concerned about the Indian problem in Texas. In other words, he saw his position as essentially a military command and did not involve himself much in domestic affairs, even though the new governor, Domingo Cabello, who replaced Ripperdá, reported directly to him. As a result of his tour, De Croix determined to reduce, if he could not halt completely, the Apache depredations. He understood more thoroughly than any commander before him the relationship of the Comanches and their allies to the Apache raids. At a council of war in Monclova in December 1777 after hearing various reports and advice, he concluded that a general campaign should be instigated against the Apaches.

In January 1778 the most important conference of the Spanish period on Texas Indian affairs was held at San Antonio. There the details of the Apache war were hammered out. After the Texas trip ended, a third Indian council was held in Chihuahua City in June and July 1778. The final strategy was simple: The Lipans and Mescaleros, already beginning to be split by the wedge of Comanche intrusion, were to be separated and a vigorous war was to be pursued against the Lipans. The heart of De Croix's strategy was to make use of the Comanches against the Lipans.

To win Comanche friendship and provoke them into war, De Croix, himself a Frenchman, depended upon another Frenchman in Spanish service. Athanase de Mézières, an accomplished officer in the French army in Louisiana, had elected to remain at Natchitoches after the transfer of territorial jurisdiction to Spain. As had so many of his brethren, he had switched his loyalties to Spain. He had married the daughter of Louis Juchereau de St. Denis, and under his father-in-law's masterful tutelage had entered the Indian trade. His abilities and his experiences with the "northern" tribes made him the ideal man to negotiate Comanche friendship.

Even before De Croix's new policy was initiated, De Mézières had made trips up the Red River as far as the Taovayas village for Alejandro O'Reilly, the new Louisiana governor—an Irish immigrant like his cousin Hugo Oconor. In February 1778 at San Antonio he received specific instructions from De Croix to visit the various Comanche bands to give presents to the chiefs and to persuade them to take the warpath against the Lipans. De Mézières was an effective diplomat, and De Croix's plan became a reality.

Relentless Comanche warriors, with the blessings of Spain as conferred by the French envoy, carried hostilities deep into Lipan territory. Reports of running fights and fierce skirmishes began to filter into San Antonio and Chihuahua during 1779 and 1780. By the latter part of 1780 various Lipan chiefs began to make their appearances at San Antonio to ask Spanish aid—and to accept a Spanish truce. De Croix instructed Governor Cabello to receive the Lipan overtures generously, to distribute presents, and to encourage the chiefs to migrate south—where, the cunning De Croix thought, they would buffer Comanche raids into northern Mexico. For De Croix knew that at best the Comanches would prove fickle allies.

But the new Indian policy worked, and there was an uneasy peace along the western frontier of Texas for several decades. With a few exceptions in later years, particularly Juan Bautista de Anza's campaign against some western Comanches in 1779, friendship with the Comanches and the other northern tribes remained the keystone of Spanish Indian policy to the end of the era. As late as 1806-1807 when the American Zebulon Pike entered the territory, the primary Spanish concern over his activities was whether he had disturbed the northern alliances. The 1808-1809 expedition of Francisco Amangual was ordered out specifically to investigate. When the first Missouri traders began to drift into New Mexico a decade or so later, Governor Melgares, a veteran of Indian affairs on the frontier, immediately reacted to the possibility that the Indian alliances were being tampered with. All of which only indicates that this new Indian policy developed by De Croix in 1778 on his tour of Texas came to be of the utmost importance to the Spanish frontier hierarchy.

All in all, however, Spanish officials had little understanding of the Indians in Texas. One can view the natives from Spanish eyes two centuries ago by seeing them as Father Morfí and Father Solís saw them. The following descriptions, taken loosely from their reports, reflect a uniform prejudice.

The Karankawa Indians were cowardly, very cruel, vile, and treacherous. They generally wandered about individually, living on the coastal islands during the summer and seeking shelter from winter weather on the mainland. They fished in Matagorda Bay (Bahía del Espíritu Santo) when they could. They frequently gathered on an island (unidentifiable) at the mouth of the Colorado where they had collected the wreckage that had washed ashore of ships lost in the Gulf—bells, pots, anchors, and so forth. They treated human survivors of such misfortunes with barbarous cruelty.

Many of the Karankawas spoke Spanish, having lived briefly and intermittently at the La Bahía mission.

Solís wrote concerning the Karankawa and allied coastal bands that they were greedy and gluttonous, eating meat so little cooked that it dripped with raw blood. Savage and emphatically lazy, they preferred to suffer hunger, nakedness (oh, shame!), and the inclemencies of weather so that they could remain free to roam indolently along the beaches and to give themselves over to all kinds of excesses, especially lust and dancing. They were particularly fond of ceremonial dances they called *mitotes*. Instrumental rhythm was produced from such items as a French pot, a tortoise shell, half of a calabash gourd, a kind of flute made from dried reeds, or a sort of tambourine-like instrument. The "music" emitted by various combinations of these instruments was accompanied by dreadful and unnatural shrieks. Dancers wriggled about in a strange fashion, occasionally jumping and leaping and making grimaces and gestures. The *mitotes* encircled a great fire and lasted three days. Men did the dancing, painted with red and black colors, with rings drawn around their blood-shot (as Solís said) eyes. Women watched, with their hair pulled down over their eyes, uttering mournful cries.

Neither Solís nor Morfí commented on the alleged cannibalism of the Karankawas, although Solís described a *mitote* in which a victim, a defeated enemy, was tied to a stake. While he burned in the center fire, the dancers leaped about in a circle making many terrible gestures, uttering sad and unnatural cries, and dashing toward the victim from time to time to slice off a part of his flesh. This they would baste in the fire and gobble down. According to Solís it was this bloody vivisection that killed the hapless victim rather than heat and suffocation. They would then cut off the skull to be mounted on a stick triumphantly and dismember the body, passing the bones around to be gnawed on. Sometimes they hung victims by the feet to roast them and then devoured the entire body.

The Karankawas and their kinsmen were filthy and smelled horrible. They were fond, said Solís, of all that was foul and pestiferous, even delighting in the odor and flesh of polecats. They pierced their ears and nose for ornamentation and decorated themselves with shells, beads, and feathers.

Their sex life must have been wild, if the celibate padres' reporting was reliable. The men sold their wives for a horse, gun, powder, bullets, beads, or anything they admired. They frequently traded their wives for those of other men and sometimes even loaned them to friends to use. Through all this atrocious abuse, said Solís, the women remained very modest. Their loins were always decently covered by loincloths, although the men ran around stark naked. The priests also commented upon the prevalance of homosexuality. Homosexual men were taken on campaigns when women were left behind and were abused in ways that the padres said were immoral.

Solís particularly had more to say about these coastal Indians than the other tribes. Morfí made more diverse observations. For instance, up the coast between the Trinity and the Neches lived the Orcoquisas and the Attacapas. They were few in number, had no fixed homes, did not cultivate the soil, did not fight or bear arms, and were of little importance.

The Xaranames were cowardly, vile, and nomadic—unworthy of notice but for the cruelties they practiced upon Europeans who chanced among them unprotected. Some apostate Xaranames had run away from mission life to live among the Tawakoni (or Tehuacana). These Indians lived in villages along the Brazos, practiced agriculture, and were industrious, docile, and friendly.

The Bidais were lazy and listless, had been greatly reduced in numbers by a smallpox epidemic, and were not dangerous except that their long-standing friendship with Lipan Apaches required that they be treated with caution. Solís visited a small band of Bidais at the time of a total eclipse of the moon; they became so frightened that they begged the priest to baptize them. "I am convinced," said he cynically, "that their fervor will be short-lived."

The Caddoan speaking Indians of East Texas were divided into different tribes, variously designated, said Morfí, as Hasinai, Tejas, Nacogdoches, etc. Morfí found only eighty warriors among the Tejas, fewer than forty among the Nabedache, and about three hundred in the Nacogdoche village. Only twenty families in all lived in the Ais village. All of the Caddoans lived an advanced village life and had complex social and religious institutions. Both priests condemned them for the worship of false gods, but Morfí found them generally friendly and industrious, while Solís disparaged them. The Indians of the Ais tribe, he commented, were the worst in the entire province of Texas. They were indolent, bold, and shameless—addicted to drunkenness, dishonesty, dancing, and especially to lust.

The Tonkawas were a wandering nation of about three hundred warriors. They were daring thieves, and Morfí believed them to be chiefly responsible for the San Sabá massacre. He believed, however, that their friendship and alliance was being won by the Spaniards.

The Comanches, who were in fact responsible for the treacherous attack on San Sabá, were reluctantly admired by Morfí. His brief comment on these Indians is almost diametrically different from all other descriptions. He reported that they were far superior to all other Indians in the province (which they were); that they were modest in dress and demeanor; that they were hospitable to visitors and kind to captives; and that they were valorous in battle. Morfí, of course, had no first-hand knowledge and but a few secondary reports. Neither Solís nor Morfí attempted to describe the Apaches, except to comment on their hostility.

Morfí, although he did not visit the Taovayas village on Red River, described it at some length. There were nearly 160 houses on both sides of the river; each house had from eight to ten beds; the total number of these Wichita speaking people was over 800. They dressed like proper Indians in long deerskin shirts, pants, leggings, and moccasins. They were industrious, planted a variety of crops, hunted, and fished. According to Morfí they irrigated from the river. They were democratic, including even women in their councils. The women did do almost all of the work of the village, while the men devoted themselves exclusively to the hunt and to war. They had some ridiculous superstitions for a religion. These Taovayas, said Morfí who had never met one personally, were cheerful, affable, docile, compassionate, respectful, generous, and kind. Paragons indeed of all the European virtues, their only fault was excessive cruelty to prisoners of war—a form of reprisal, apologized the priest, not a mark of natural cruelty.

The priests' observations of the Texas Indians are almost totally worthless from an ethnological view. They do present, however, what must have been the general opinion of the Spaniards toward the natives at about the time of American Independence. It is worth noting that with almost no exception, those Indians with whom the Spaniards had actual contact were considered savage, dishonest, and lazy, as well, of course, as utterly deprived of Christian morals. Those Indians of whom they had little first-hand knowledge were cast somewhat in the romantic pastoral tradition of European ideals.

MAP 5

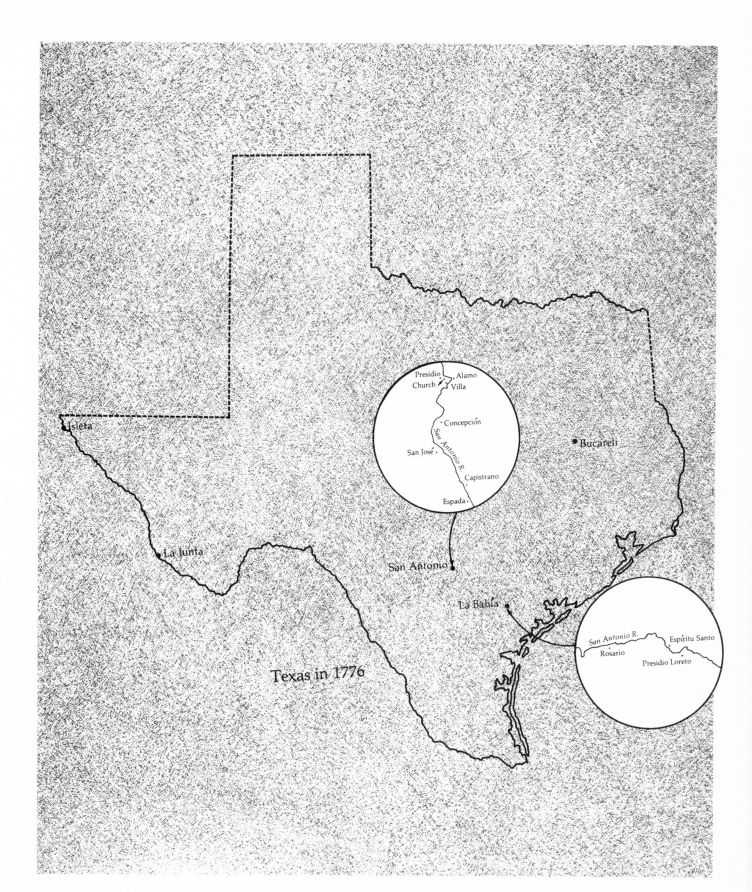

Texas in 1776

Isleta

La Junta

San Antonio

La Bahía

Bucareli

Presidio Church · Alamo · Villa

· Concepción

San Antonio R.

San José ·

· Capistrano

Espada

San Antonio R. · Espíritu Santo

Rosario · Presidio Loreto

TEXAS IN 1776

6

In 1776 the present area of the state of Texas was thinly popu-
lated by Indians and even more sparsely settled by Spaniards. The
western plains were dominated by bands of nomadic hunters, princi-
pally Lipan Apaches and their mortal enemies, the Comanches. Their
territory was infringed upon by seminomads, such as the Tonkawas
and Tehuacanas, who lived in *rancherías* in the central part of the
state and did some farming. The best-known Indian settlement of the
time was the Taovayas village on Red River, where Indians, Frenchmen, and Spaniards had traded under a native commercial truce for
decades. Blighted remnants of the once powerful Caddoan tribes still
lived in villages in the piney woods, but their culture was in decay for
a variety of reasons, not the least of which was their more intimate
relations with Europeans than the other Indians. Along the gulf
various bands of coastal Indians, from the pacific Orcoquisas north of
Galveston Bay to the savage Karankawas along the southern coast,

eked out a beachcombing existence. They seemed to be neither hurt nor hindered by Spanish contact, especially the Karankawas who fifty years later were to plague the Austin colonists. Numerous little bands of primitive Coahuiltecan Indians roamed South Texas, hunting small game, rooting and grubbing, and eating wild nuts and berries. Impermanent, shifting, merging one band into another, they made little impression on the Spaniards of the time and had all but disappeared by the end of the century. But these people were the only Texas natives with whom the Spanish mission system had had any success at all. Some of the Coahuiltecans from the San Antonio area had adapted to mission life. Perhaps they were so weak or had so few or such flexible cultural patterns that they did not resist reduction as did the other Texas Indians.

The Spanish settlements in the present area of Texas were truly oases of civilization and Christianity in the vast and largely semiarid wilderness. On the present Texas side of the Rio Grande, and clinging to the river for sustenance, were Isleta, just downstream from Paso del Norte; the tenuous settlement at La Junta (present Presidio); and the village of Laredo. None of these was considered a part of the Spanish province of Texas. There was a moderately prosperous island of settlement at San Antonio, the capital, where there were five missions, a garrison, a villa, and a few outlying ranches. At the Cibolo crossing of the road to La Bahía there was a small detachment of troops and a few refugees from East Texas. Scattered ranches dotted the San Antonio River valley as far as La Bahía. There an imposing presidio and two missions had stood for about a quarter of a century. Newly founded Bucareli, 150 miles away, trembled on the banks of the Trinity, a village of perhaps two or three hundred souls. An unknown and uncounted number of people unquestionably still remained illegally in the piney woods of the abandoned East Texas mission field.

Isleta had been established when the Pueblo Indians of New Mexico revolted against their Spanish overlords in 1680 and drove them from the upper Rio Grande in New Mexico. The refugees from this terrifying uprising—nearly half the Hispanicized peoples were murdered—fled southward in panic. Many stopped at El Paso del Norte to establish a new Spanish foothold in the Southwest. The principal settlements were on the south side of the Rio Grande in the present Juarez valley. However, two priests and a handful of Tigua Indians, fleeing from the massacre at the Tigua Pueblo near present Albuquerque where the Mission Corpus Christi de Isleta had been built, set themselves up across the river from the other settlements at El Paso del Norte. Giving their new settlement the same name, Isleta, they became the first permanent Hispanic residents of present Texas. In 1776 Isleta consisted of a small church, some scattered mud huts for the Tigua Indians, and fields irrigated from the Rio Grande. Its size is unknown, but it was small, unimportant, and relatively isolated despite the fact that it was only about twenty miles from the major settlement of El Paso del Norte (present Juarez) across the river.

There is, in fact, no clear evidence regarding the main channel of the Rio Grande, either at the time of the establishment of Isleta or in 1776. Inferential evidence from the diary of Juan Dominguez de Mendoza in 1684 would indicate that Isleta was on the north or left bank. So did Pedro de Rivera locate it in 1726. However, Lafora described almost a continuous settlement on the right bank for about twenty miles downstream from El Paso del Norte, including the town of San Antonio de Isleta. But his map showed Isleta was on the right bank. Despite this confusion of two hundred years, Isleta is today a part of the modern Texas city of El Paso.

Two other settlements which had been established on the south bank of the Rio Grande are now in Texas because of the erratic nature of the Rio Grande: Socorro and San Elizario. Nuestra Señora de la Concepción del Socorro was established in 1682, like Isleta, as a mission for loyal refugees from the Pueblo Revolt. It had been secularized in 1756 but could not support itself as a parish church. In 1771 during the reorganization of the Franciscan jurisdiction, it was restored to the control of the order. Thus, in 1776 it was a sister mission to Isleta but was at that time across the river and a few miles downstream. San Elizario had been established in 1772 with Oconor's implementation of the New Regulations. A presidio of that name was built at or near the site of the present town, and a small settlement grew up around it. After the presidio was removed in 1814 the little village remained. Floods in the early nineteenth century changed the course of the Rio Grande to put both San Elizario and Socorro on the same side of the river as Isleta.

Far downstream, near the tip of the curve in the Rio known as the Big Bend, was another settlement. Its history and exact location are obscured by time and inadequate research. Until recent years historians of the Spanish era have stated that it was called Presidio del Norte and was located on the Texas side of the river near present Presidio, Texas. More recent research together with archeological excavation indicate that it was across the river near present Ojinaga, Mexico. This area, where the Conchas River of Mexico flows northeastward into the Rio Grande, was a strategic location known generally as La Junta. A presidio, originally named Nuestra Señora de Belén y Santiago de Amarilla, was established there in 1757. Later moved away, it was returned to La Junta pursuant to the New Regulations and rebuilt in 1773. Commonly called at that time Presidio El Norte, its location was clearly on the Mexican side of the river. However, there was probably some livestock raising by civilians on the Texas side of the La Junta area in 1776. Like the presidio at San Elizario, at the time El Norte had a military complement of about sixty troops.

It is worth noting that Rubí had chosen the Rio Grande as the defensive rim of northern Mexico and had ordered the presidios defending it to be located on the south side of the river. From El Paso del Norte to the mouth of the river there were no settlements on the north side of the river except for Isleta and Laredo.

Laredo had been established by José de Escandón in 1755 as one of the 23 towns he had founded in Nuevo Santander. Only two of these, Laredo and Dolores, were located north of the Rio Grande. Dolores soon disappeared, but Laredo hung onto existence tenaciously. Both Lafora and Solís reported a small settlement there, with people living on both sides of the river. Neither recorded a mission, but Solís gave the name of the resident priest as José (or Joseph) Gutiérrez. Lafora stated that there were sixty huts on both sides of the river and that the villagers formed an armed militia commanded by a captain under orders of the governor of Nuevo Santander.

The boundary between Texas and Nuevo Santander, which became the Mexican state of Tamaulipas, was the Nueces River from its mouth to the crossing of the road from San Juan Bautista to San Antonio. West of that road the boundary between Coahuila and Texas had not been defined. But if one followed that road northward from the Rio Grande in 1776, at some point he would be in Texas, and further along, he would reach the provincial capital at San Antonio.

Here was the center of life in colonial Texas. Just over a half century old at that time, it had been in reality the keystone of Spanish settlement since its establishment by Father Olivares and Captain Martín de Alarcón in 1718. In name Los Adaes was the capital and to the Spanish bureaucracy, San Antonio was merely a halfway station on the road to Los Adaes. But the Chicken War of 1719 had sent the

East Texans scurrying back to San Antonio. At that time there were but a half dozen civilian families, about twenty soldiers working on the construction of the San Antonio de Bexar presidio, and a couple of priests at the site of the recently consecrated Mission San Antonio de Valero, soon to be generally known as the Alamo.

Chagrined priests moved a few miles to the south and dedicated a new mission, San José y San Miguel de Aguayo—named in honor of the new governor and captain general of Texas. Just over a decade later, in 1731, three of the East Texas missions were relocated at San Antonio, and a small settlement of immigrants from the Canary Islands was established. The Canary Islanders were under official auspices, were given land grants, and were allowed to establish a town with *villa* status, that is, having some privileges of self-government. Sites for the three missions, following an abortive attempt to relocate on the Colorado, were consecrated south of the town, and the names of the missions were changed. The original San Francisco de los Tejas became San Francisco de la Espada. San José de los Nazonis became San Juan Capistrano (a half century before the California home of the swallows was built). And Purísima Concepción de los Hainai became Purísima Concepción de Acuña. These three missions, like the Valero or Alamo Mission, were operated by Franciscans from the *colegio* at Querétero. San José y San Miguel de Aguayo was a Zacatecan mission.

By the middle of the eighteenth century the five missions in the San Antonio area had approximately their present shapes and facades. Importing reduced Indians from Mexico and missionizing the docile Coahuiltecan bands in the region, the missions of San Antonio enjoyed considerable success and a degree of prosperity, although they never became completely self-supporting. The padres built *acequias* to carry water to fields that they irrigated. They established and maintained herds of sheep and cattle. Inside the mission walls they built hutments for the Indians and trained them in the arts and crafts of civilization. In 1772 the four Queréteran missions were transferred to the Zacatecan fathers. At that time San José was the largest and most successful; the Alamo was far and away the least prosperous.

All were at their present sites and largely in their present form in 1776. San Francisco de la Espada was the farthest from town, about twelve miles downstream on the San Antonio River. San Juan Capistrano was on the river, about two miles closer to town. San

José was next and about a half mile west of the river. Concepción was near the juncture of San Pedro Creek with the river, two and a half miles south of the Alamo. The main part of the town was about one-half mile west of the Alamo, with the crumbling presidio and governor's quarters on the east side of San Pedro Creek. An extraordinarily good description of these places as they must have appeared in 1776 can be obtained from Morfí's observations of 1778.

The presidio, originally built of stone and adobe, was almost in ruins. It was surrounded by a poor stockade on which a few swivel guns were mounted. They were useless except for firing blank charges of powder for salutes. When Baron Ripperdá brought his bride to San Antonio in 1770 his first quarters were the best billets in the presidio—the garrison jail. A portion of the presidio in time became what is known today as the Governors' Palace. Lafora's 1767 sketch shows the guardhouse on the west end of the north side of the presidio quadrangle. The captain's quarters were on the west side about where the Governors' Palace is today. Between the crumbling garrison which housed about fifty men and the squalid but grandly named Villa de San Fernando de Bexar stood the parish church whose priest also served as chaplain for the troops. Morfí found the church structure spacious, with a vaulted roof, but so poorly built he did not think it would stand very long. It didn't, but on its site today rises the beautiful San Fernando Cathedral.

The town consisted of fifty-nine stone and adobe or mud houses and seventy-nine wooden huts. All were so crude that the settlement more resembled a peasant pueblo than a villa and provincial capital. There was no organized plan, the crooked, meandering streets being torturous when dry and muddy bogs after a rain. The civilian population, which must have numbered between four and five hundred, was made up of *isleños*, families of the Canary Islanders, and of *familias de pais*, or country families. Although it is not certain, this latter group seems to have consisted of mestizos of varying degrees of native origin, most of whom probably had migrated from Mexico.

About a half mile ("two gun shots' distance") east of the presidio stood the Alamo on the east bank of the bend of the San Antonio River and across the stream from the presidio and the town. It consisted at the time of Morfí's visit of a small convent about 150 feet square, two stories tall, forming an inner courtyard. The rooms of this structure were for the missionaries and included a porter's lodge, a kitchen, a refectory, and offices. The original chapel had fallen in ruins shortly after its construction. A visiting inspector in 1762 commented that a new chapel was under construction. It was still under construction when Morfí visited it, and services were being held in the sacristy. Indian quarters formed a square, one story high, about the chapel and the convent. Included in the mission establishment was a large weaving room with four looms and a number of spinning wheels. There were also a workshop and two other rooms for storing tools and wool. An *acequia* brought water inside the walls of the mission, and a watch tower surmounted the entrance to the convent proper. Morfí did not give the population of the mission but stated that the number of Indian families was "greatly reduced" from the 76 families reported in 1762. The weaving work had been abandoned, and there were scarcely enough Indians at the mission to tend the fields.

Nor did Morfí give the number of Indians at Purísima Concepción, stating only that it, too, was greatly reduced since the 1762 report which had listed 58 families. The mission however was handsome. Indian quarters running back in two parallel rows from a convent formed a square, the back side of which was enclosed by a granary. The chapel was beautiful, approximately 60 feet by 20 feet, built of stone, with a vaulted roof and two bell towers.

Mission San José, said Morfí, was truthfully the first mission in America in beauty, plan, and strength. Father Solís had commented in 1768 that he could not find the words to describe its beauty. A somewhat later visitor in 1785, Father José Francisco López, wrote that the church and the sacristy at San José had the most beautiful architecture north of Saltillo. These comments were made even before the addition of the renowned "Rose Window" in the 1790's. Today they are echoed by thousands of visitors to the restored mission which is a National Historic Monument.

An approximation of how San José looked about the time of American Independence can be derived from the three careful descriptions of Solís (1768), Morfí (1778), and López (1785).

The living quarters and offices formed a near square 216 by 220 varas (600 by 611 feet), with the Indian quarters, whose backs formed the outside perimeter walls, being 4 varas (ca. 11 feet) deep. There were four gates, one in each wall and each with good strong locks. A defensive bastion was built over each gate, and small holes for weapons penetrated the rooms on both sides of the gates. In addition there were two smaller entrances, one of which opened opposite the church on the west wall and the other of which may have been made between 1778 and 1785. On diagonally opposite corners two small towers rose for defensive firing along the entire perimeter. Like all of the major structures of the mission, these walls were built of stone and mortar. There was a large granary, lime and brick kilns, a forge, and carpenter, blacksmith, and tailor shops. One room served as an armory where guns, bows and arrows, and lances were kept to arm the Indian neophytes as an auxiliary militia. In another room were stored costumes and decorations for the Indians to adorn themselves with when dancing. The dances at San José were devised by the padres, apparently based on Spanish folkdances, in order to divert the Indians from the wild, pagan *mitotes* which Solís so objected to. In short, everything that the mission community needed was within the stout, easily defended rock walls, and it all was so well planned that even in the case of a prolonged siege, the mission folk could laugh at the enemy. The granary was kept well stocked with food, and wells within the walls afforded plenty of good water. One of these wells was apparently artisian, the flow of which was directed into an *acequia* which was used to irrigate a vegetable garden.

The most striking feature of the mission was the church itself. The cornerstone for it had been laid by Hugo Oconor on May 19, 1768; at the time of Morfí's visit ten years later it was so nearly completed that he was able to describe it in considerable detail. The building was so fine a one, he wrote, that it would grace a large city as a parish church. The sandy limestone from which it was built was obtained from a quarry near the Concepción mission. As the freshly cut stone hardened it blended both structurally and harmoniously with the lime mortar. The church's facade was so heavily decorated with statues and ornaments that Morfí opined they detracted from the natural beauty. The main entrance was in the center, with a large balcony over it. Dominating the upper facade was a handsome hexagonal window which lit the choir loft inside.

The chapel and the sacristy (where mass was held in 1776 prior to the completion of the church) were valued at 30,000 pesos and the ornaments and furnishings at between 8,000 and 10,000, five times the value of any other in Texas. The priests' living quarters were adjacent, two stories high, with spacious galleries. On the lower level were the mission offices and a kitchen; the missionaries' quarters were on the second floor.

All of the visitors noted that the Indians at San José were more industrious and spoke better Spanish than those at the other missions. Morfí commented that because of their obvious prosperity they were the envy of the slovenly settlers at San Fernando. Whether so or not, the mission population declined throughout the last part of the century. Solís reported 350 persons at the mission in 1768; Morfí, who did not give a number, said the population was greatly reduced in 1778; López found a total of only 138 at the mission in 1785.

San Juan Capistrano was by no means as prosperous a mission as San José, nor even as strong as Concepción. The convent had four cells to quarter the priests, two offices, a refectory, work-shop, and kitchen. The Indian quarters, built onto the perimeter walls, were not as comfortable as those at San José. There were three entrances to the quadrangle, which was about 250 by 150 feet. None of the three visitors gave a very adequate description of the church, and archeological evidence has revealed that there were two structures that had served as chapels. The present one is the more recent and may not have existed in 1776. López in 1785 wrote that a second chapel was under construction but was unfinished. The old church is today in ruins on the east side of the quadrangle. The Indian population declined from 203 persons in 1762 to 58 in 1785.

San Francisco de la Espada, almost ill-fated from the time of its abortive establishment in 1690 in East Texas for the Tejas Indians, was in sad condition in 1776. The church, poorly built to start with, had been razed because it threatened to fall in; mass was held in another room of the compound, which had four corner towers. The convent was two stories tall—four priests' rooms above, three rooms below. There was a granary and a workshop. Everything was built of stone, but the structures were plain and poorly arranged. The Indian population was reported by Morfí as 133 in 1778, a possible error since that was probably the number in 1762.

In all, the San Antonio area, including the presidio, the village, and the five missions, had in Morfí's estimation a total population of 2,060 persons: 759 men, 613 women, 373 boys, 300 girls, 4 male slaves, and 11 female slaves. These made up 514 families. In an apparent reference to the adult male population, he said that 324 were Spanish, 268 were Indians, 16 were mestizos, and 151 were (literally) of "broken color." The reference to Spaniards was to *gentes de razones* and consequently probably did not mean men of pure

Spanish descent. The 16 mestizos were probably native, that is San Antonio, mixed bloods. The reference to "broken color" could mean almost anything since there were about a half-dozen different vernacular terms for mixtures of Negro, Indian, and Spaniard.

There were five roads leading into and away from San Antonio plus a sixth connecting road to the outlying missions. The Camino Real de Texas left town going north and then curved northeast toward East Texas. Its route out of town closely approximates the modern San Antonio street called Nacogdoches Road. There is evidence, mostly inferential, in the accounts of the period that it was not in use at the time. The Camino Real de San Sabá was never a heavily traveled trail. It had been broken for traffic to the mission and presidio near present Menard, running a twisted course to the northwest. After the presidio was abandoned and the garrison transferred, the road was completely abandoned. It was not too far from present Bandera Road but it had not left a sufficient impact on the land to become a place name in later times. Two roads, the upper and lower trails, led to the Presidio del Rio Grande at San Juan Bautista. The lower road went almost due south from town roughly along modern Laredo Street. The fifth of these roads was the most important at this time—the Camino Real de la Bahía del Espíritu Santo. Its southeasterly route from town is largely obliterated by modern north-south streets, but the name Goliad Road remains today on sections of it.

Where the road to La Bahía crossed Cibolo Creek, near the present Wilson-Karnes county line, Ripperdá had built the short-lived military post called Santa Cruz de Cíbolo. Lafora commented that a number of settlers had ranchos along Cibolo Creek and needed protection. A dozen to twenty men had been stationed at the crossing to protect San Antonio's flank as well as the western approach to La Bahía. There some of the refugee settlers from East Texas had squatted in 1773, determined to go no farther. Morfí found it to be a wretched fort with wooden stockades around it and with only seven persons there in 1778, but that was probably an underestimation.

The settlement at present Goliad—two missions and a presidio —was approximately fifty miles down this road that loosely followed the left banks of the San Antonio River. The Rosario Mission lay across the river, on the south side, about four miles west of Espíritu Santo. The mission obtained water from the river from which it also irrigated fields and had acceptable crops. No detailed description of the mission as it was in 1776 is extant and the site today is marked only by crumbling rock walls. The quarters, Morfí said, were good and comfortable. Solís, who stayed there during his visit to the area, seemed to find it more comfortable than its sister mission. The church was built of wood at that time, plastered and whitewashed, with a beamed roof and shingles placed to resemble panels. Because Morfí's account so closely follows Solís' description, one cannot help but doubt that Morfí visited Rosario personally. He did not estimate the number of Indians at the mission but merely stated that most of the neophytes had fled.

Mission Espíritu Santo was older and was built of stone. The mission quadrangle, like those at San Antonio, was rectangularly shaped, with the perimeter walls forming the back wall of Indian quarters and work rooms. Everything was built of limestone and mortar and had wooden roofs. There was a fine church building and sacristy, adjoining which was the customary convent for the missionaries. The visitors of this period who wrote about it were not particularly impressed and so supplied few details. López estimated the value of the mission and its furnishings to be 12,000 pesos or about one-sixth of the value he had placed on San José. In 1778 the mission housed about 300 Indians from various bands, but this neophyte population was not considered stable.

Across the river and downstream a short distance reared the battlements of the Loreto presidio. It, too, failed to make a sufficient impression on any of the visitors of this period to produce a useful description. According to Lafora everything was built of adobe, but the massive amount of rock work later found at the site belies this observation. His sketch shows an unfinished quadrangle about 265 by 325 feet. The captain's quarters and presidial offices were along the south end. A small chapel formed a portion of the west wall. The soldiers' quarters were shown as huts outside of the quadrangle and between it and the river. A small battery of field pieces was mounted on the west wall. The east wall was shown only partially closed in.

A magnificent reconstruction of the presidio stands today based upon the most thorough historical and archeological evidences. This was, however, a perplexing task because of the numerous bits of construction, remodeling, and rebuilding that took place from the time of its relocation at the site in 1749 to a crude attempt to restore the ruins in the 1930s. Inadequate as it is, the Lafora sketch of 1767 is probably the best representation of the way Loreto looked at the time of the American Revolution. A complement of 55 was stationed there in accordance with the New Regulations of 1772.

Bucareli in 1776 was at the mid-point and height of its brief life span, 1774 to 1778. It had at that time a score of wooden houses and numerous *jacales*, a wooden church (constructed by Gil Ybarbo's French confederate from Natchitoches), and a jail, all of which were surrounded by a stockade. A more detailed description is given in the special chapter about its establishment.

In East Texas in 1776 officially there was not supposed to be any settlement. But it is fairly obvious that there must have been anywhere from a dozen or two to perhaps over a hundred persons scattered in the region that had been Spain's initial grasp on Texas. These folk had engaged in illicit commerce with the French and the Indians from 1722 on and continued to trade in contraband after the exodus from East Texas fifty years later. There is no way to know how many were living around the abandoned missions and ranchos in 1776. Certainly all of the people at Los Adaes had not left there as ordered. Ybarbo had sequestered part of his own family and about a dozen others at his Lobanillo ranch, near present San Augustine. As soon as Bucareli was established intercourse between the exiles and Natchitoches was resumed. There must have been a fairly considerable amount of traffic between the Trinity and Red rivers during this period, with the population, legal and illegal, in a state of flux.

Such was the condition of Texas at the time of the American Declaration of Independence. It was mostly pristine wilderness, sparsely occupied by weak, primitive, and generally declining Indian bands, and spottily settled by a few islands of Spanish civilization. Small and scattered as they were, these tiny Spanish settlements should neither be pitied nor ridiculed. Just as the British colonies along the coast were entering a new and glorious era in 1776, so were the Spanish settlements in Texas. The shift in Spanish imperial policy and the reorganization of governmental jurisdiction were to bring a period of moderate expansion and better times, if not true prosperity, to Texas. And from this, the heritage of colonial Spain was forever to enrich the culture of Texas.

EPILOGUE

7

In 1779 there was a shortage of beef in Louisiana. This had probably happened before and may, in fact, have been a chronic condition. But no one had done anything about it before. In 1779 the energetic and influential Bernardo de Gálvez was governor of Louisiana. He requested permission to buy beef cattle in Texas, where there were so many cows nobody knew what to do with them, and drive them overland to Louisiana. Domingo Cabello was the newly appointed governor of Texas, reporting at that time directly to the commander of the Interior Provinces, who was none other than the competent and progressive Teodoro de Croix. Permission was granted. The result changed the history of Texas and ultimately shaped the destiny of western North America.

It was as if Gálvez had touched a spark to a powder keg. Every element, save one, of a booming cattle business had already emerged in Texas. The cattle were there, by the thousands of head.

The techniques for handling them had been developed, almost to perfection. The vaqueros to use the techniques were available, for the most part without any other employment. And the horses for them to ride had been trained to work with cattle, from the time they had been broken. The missing element was a viable market for beef. Permission to supply Louisiana's need started a boom.

Gálvez's agent bought over fifteen hundred head around San Antonio. The first long trail drive to market followed the tortuous road to East Texas that Rubí and Solís had taken, through forests and over rivers that would have caused most nineteenth century trail bosses to turn back. But the drive was an immense success, despite the incredible effort it must have taken. Profits to be derived from selling Texas cattle in Louisiana were quickly apparent. To a people without any financial prospects at all, it mattered little how much work it was to drive the cow-beasts through the woods. To a province without any previous economic base whatsoever, the Louisiana cattle market was a miracle.

The rush was on. The next summer three herds totaling nearly five thousand head were successfully trailed up the Camino Real and across the swamps to Louisiana. The next year the number probably doubled, and in the years that followed, official estimates of the cattle trailed to Louisiana came to about fifteen thousand annually. This did not include the number driven illegally on which the inevitable government fees had not been paid. Some illegal drovers got caught; others did not. The frequent trials of those who did indicate that a substantial number of untaxed animals must be added to the official estimates.

No historian has yet traced the effects this sudden economic windfall may have had on Texas, but they must have been considerable. Nacogdoches, the extralegal refuge of the Adaesaños, prospered and was legalized. Ephemeral settlements sprang up at the Trinity crossing and at the Atascosito crossing of the Colorado. One can only speculate about the expansion of ranching along the San Antonio River where it had gotten its start. But Texas' growth was soon aborted; the end came in 1803 when the United States acquired Louisiana and a short-sighted Spanish bureaucracy shut off the legal cattle trade. It was in those two decades, however, that the foundations of the great western range cattle industry were laid. After the American Civil War, cattlemen and drovers, using the techniques of the vaqueros, spread this heritage of colonial Spain across the plains of North America all the way to Canada.

It had been the new and vital administration of De Croix and the Interior Provinces that had made the development possible. Bureaucratic dryrot soon developed. De Croix was rewarded by promotion to the highest position in the New World, viceroy of Peru. His successor in 1783, a competent officer who had served under him, Felipe de Neve, died a year later. Soon the independent unit was subordinated to the command of the viceroy and broken into three impotent subdivisions. The effect of this administrative mistake was not felt immediately because the viceroy at that time was Bernardo de Gálvez, but decadence in the northern bureaucracy was his successor.

Gálvez had been given the post of viceroy in 1785 partially because of the influence of his uncle. But while still governor of Louisiana he had taken another action that was to have an enduring effect on Texas. He had sponsored a survey of the Gulf coast. The navigator in charge was José de Evia, about whom unfortunately nothing else is known; unfortunately, because he was responsible for an inexplicable linguistic anomaly. In honor of his patron he gave the large bay into which the Trinity River disembogued the name *Bahía de Galveston.* There is no reasonable explanation for this semantic curiosity: "ton" is an English suffix for "town"; it is not now and was not in the eighteenth century a meaningful suffix in Spanish. The only usage of "ton" in modern Spanish is in an idiomatic expression, *sin ton ni son,* meaning (most appropriately) "without rhyme or reason." Thus, contrary to general belief, the suffix "ton" was added to the name "Gálvez" in 1785; the island, then called "Isla de Culebras," later became known as Galveston Island; there was no town there until M. B. Menard laid out Galveston City in 1838.

Following the break up of the Interior Provinces in 1786, while Gálvez was viceroy, attempts were made to tie Texas closer to the other Spanish frontier provinces. Pedro (or Pierre) Vial, another Frenchman in the service of Spain, was commissioned to explore a route from San Antonio to Santa Fe. Leaving San Antonio in 1786, he spent several weeks visiting the Tawakoni ranchería in Central Texas and the Taovayas village on Red River. Then, traveling with a band of friendly Comanche Indians, he crossed the plains to New Mexico, entering Santa Fe in 1787. The next year he explored a route from the New Mexican capital directly to Natchitoches in Louisiana while his corporal, José Mares, led another party back across Texas to San Antonio. Vial returned to San Antonio and tried to find a more practical route to Santa Fe in 1789, but the nature of the country foreordained there would be no traffic across the plains.

Partially because of the brief economic prosperity in Texas, the authorities decided that the missions at San Antonio could be secularized. This meant taking them out of the jurisdiction of the regular or monastic clergy—the Franciscans in Texas—and placing them under the secular hierarchy as parish churches in the bishopric of Nuevo León. As missions, they had been a constant drain on the treasury; as parish churches they might become self-sustaining through church taxes and parishioners' tithes. Such secularization was the goal of the mission effort. It came to Texas in 1794, although the missions around La Bahía (Espíritu Santo, Rosario, and Refugio which was established in 1793) were exempt. Secularization in Texas was a failure. The few Indians remaining at the missions wandered off; the few civilians living around them could not support parishes; the missions were for all practical purposes abandoned and fell into decay. The Alamo, because of its location in town, was used as a hospital and adjunct for the garrison. It too fell into a semiruined condition.

Soon after the turn of the new century Texas slid gently into a somnambulant pastoral existence. This decline was due partially to the decadence of the Spanish bureaucracy of that period and partially to the decision of the officials to stop the cattle trade with Louisiana. Thus, after a brief renaissance at the time of the American Revolution, Texas dozed until the future stirred it.

BIBLIOGRAPHY

Bolton, Herbert Eugene. Texas in the middle eighteenth century: studies in Spanish colonial administration. Berkeley (Univ. of California), 1915. Reprinted New York (Russell and Russell), 1962.

Castañeda, Carlos E. Our Catholic heritage in Texas, 1519-1936. 7 vols. Austin (Von Boeckmann-Jones and Knights of Columbus), 1936-1958.

Faulk, Odie B. The leather jacket soldiers: Spanish military equipment and institutions of the late 18th century. Pasadena (Socio-Technical), 1971.

_____ and Sidney Brinckerhoff. Lancers for the king: a study of the frontier military system of northern New Spain. With a translation of the Royal Regulations of 1772. Phoenix (Ariz. Hist. Foundation), 1965.

Kinnaird, Lawrence. The frontiers of New Spain: Nicolás de Lafora's description, 1766-1768. Albuquerque (Quivera Society), 1958.

López, José Francisco. The Texas missions in 1785. Trans. by J. Autrey Dobbs. Austin (Knights of Columbus), 1940. Preliminary Studies of the Texas Catholic Hist. Soc., vol. 3, no. 6.

Morfí, Juan Agustín. History of Texas, 1673-1779. Trans. by Carlos E. Castañeda. 2 vols. Albuquerque (Quivera Soc.), 1935.

Moorhead, Max L. The presidio: bastion of the Spanish borderlands. Norman (Univ. of Okla.), 1975.

Pichardo, José Antonio. Treatise on the limits of Louisiana and Texas. . . . Trans. and ed. by Charles W. Hackett. 4 vols. Austin (Univ. of Texas), 1931-1946.

Schuetz, Mardith K. Historic background of the mission San Antonio de Valero. Austin (State Building Commission Archeological Program, Report no. 1), 1966.

_____. The history and archeology of mission San Juan Capistrano. 2 vols. Austin (State Building Commission Archeological Program, Report no. 10), 1968.

Solís, José de. The Solís diary of 1767. Trans. by Peter P. Forrestal. Austin (Knights of Columbus), 1931. Preliminary Studies of the Texas Catholic Hist. Soc., vol. 1, no. 6.

Thomas, Alfred Barnaby. Teodoro de Croix and the northern frontier of New Spain, 1776-1783. Norman (Univ. of Okla.), 1941.

Tunnell, Curtis D., and W. W. Newcomb. A Lipan Apache mission: San Lorenzo de Santa Cruz, 1762-1771. Austin (Texas Memorial Museum, Bltn. 14), 1969.

Winfrey, Dorman, and others. Six missions of Texas. Waco (Texian), 1965.

Vigness, David M. "Don Hugo Oconor and New Spain's northeastern frontier, 1764-1776," Journal of the West, VI (1967), 27-40.

INDEX

Seymour V. Connor has long been one of the leading authorities on Texas history about which he has written extensively. Among his books are *The Peters Colony of Texas; A Biggers Chronicle; Adventure in Glory; A Preliminary Guide to the Archives of Texas; Texas: A History; Texas: The Twenty-eighth Star;* and *North America Divided: The Mexican War 1846-48.* He has edited *The Texas Treasury Papers; Builders of the Southwest; The Saga of Texas; Dear America; The West Is For Us;* and *Politics in the West.*

His twelfth grade text book on Texas is currently in use in over half the high schools in the state, and his college-level text is in broad use throughout the Southwest. Recipient of several historical awards, he is also a life Fellow and Past President of the Texas State Historical Association and is listed in *Who's Who in America* and *Who's Who in the South and Southwest.* He is a professor of history at Texas Tech University.